soft furnishings

for living rooms

First published 2002

© Miriam Coe 2002

Illustrations by Miriam Coe and Brian Flynn
All jacket and interior photography by Michael Wicks except for the following:
title page, pages 88 and 112 by Lizzie Orme; pages 5, 12, 42, 108–9 by Tino Tedaldi;
pages 6, 84 and 87 by Russell Sadur.

ISBN 0 7134 8041 6

A CIP catalogue record for this book is available from the British Library.

Printed in Kyodo Printing Co. Pte Ltd, Singapore.

for the publishers

B T Batsford
64 Brewery Road
London N7 9NT
England
www.batsford.com

A member of Chrysalis Books plc

soft furnishings
for living rooms

miriam coe

B T Batsford • London

To all my students,

who have taught me so much.

Miriam Coe, 2002

Contents

Introduction

At some stage most of us are lucky enough to have some space to call our own, even if it is only one room. The nesting instinct is strong and we find ourselves needing to feather our nests. It is very natural to want our surroundings to look and feel comfortable. To have other people do this for us is a very expensive process, so to do it for ourselves can save a lot of money. Making your own soft furnishings is also fun to do and satisfies a creative need within us which we all have and which, due to lack of opportunity in modern lifestyles, is not always expressed. Sadly, many people are not taught how to make things for themselves now and instead, they look to classes and books for help and inspiration.

This book is designed to take the student through a carefully structured programme, starting with the very simplest and moving on to the more advanced projects within each section. The projects themselves have been carefully chosen to give a mix of traditional and modern techniques. We begin with window treatments, which could be said to be the most important soft furnishings in a room. Here, we start with a simple sheer curtain (drape), which could equally well be made in a thicker fabric if required – the technique would still be the same. We move on to a more advanced lined curtain and then to the ultimate interlined curtain. A Roman blind (shade) is also included within this section as an alternative to curtains.

The next chapter deals with accessories for windows, again starting with a very basic throw-over swag, progressing to more advanced swags and tails. Also included within this chapter are tiebacks, again starting with the simplest and moving on to more complicated plaited designs. We then look at covers. Once again we start with the simplest, yet most effective and stylish throw, which is so versatile and can be used to cover almost anything, and end with a very tailored and seemingly complicated loose cover. Cushions (pillows) are such fun to make and the final project chapter is devoted to them. Again, we begin with the simplest square cushion and move on through different fasteners, zips (zippers), buttons and ties, before tackling three-dimensional cushions in the form of a bolster and a box cushion. In this chapter we also show you how to make tassels and cords to decorate your work.

Once you have worked your way through this course you should feel confident enough to tackle any soft furnishing project for the living room. Happy sewing!

Miriam Coe.

Miriam Coe

Getting started

Y ou do not need a lot of specialist equipment to make soft furnishings. In fact, you probably have most of the things listed below. However, if you need to start from scratch, try to buy the best tools you can afford and cherish them. They will become your friends and last for years.

Basic equipment

Tape measure

A reliable tape measure is essential. It needs to be of good quality and must be renewed frequently as tape measures do have a tendency to stretch with age and become inaccurate. I have often seen people with ones that have missing inches at the beginning. This is asking for trouble! For measuring windows for blinds (shades) and curtains (drapes), a fabric tape measure is not as accurate or as easy to use as a metal tape.

Metre rule or yardstick

This is another very useful measuring instrument. Available in plastic or wood, they are equally good. They must be kept clean and free from splinters.

T-square

This is very useful for determining right angles and so straightening up the cut edge of the fabric.

Marking equipment

There are various markers available, ranging from special pens whose lines fade in daylight to crayons of various colours. Yet it's hard to beat the traditional tailor's chalk, which comes in square and triangular shapes. Several colours are available, but white is the easiest to remove. This can be done with a brush.

Tailor's chalk needs to be sharpened regularly to give an accurate line. The blade of the scissors can be used for this.

Pins

I like extra fine, extra long pins for general use but occasionally, when using bulky fabrics or many thicknesses, very long, coloured headed pins are stronger and easier to see. Always throw away any blunt or rusty pins immediately as they could spoil the fabric.

Needles

There are several different types of hand sewing needles, all with their own specific uses. They come in a variety of sizes – the higher the number, the finer the needle.

Sharps are needles that have been designed for general purpose sewing. They are a medium length with small rounded eyes. Sometimes I find I need a finer needle,

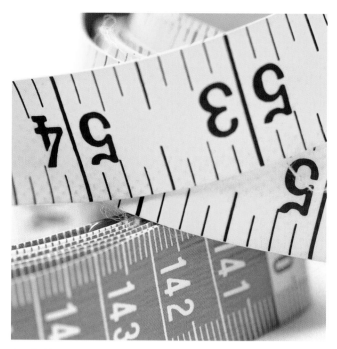

A reliable tape measure is essential.

which punctures certain fabrics more easily. I then choose 'straws', which are very fine and yet long. For intricate hand work, 'betweens' are the best choice as they are both small and fine, making tiny stitches much easier.

Needles do become blunt and they can then damage the fabric. Throw away any blunt or rusty needles immediately.

Thimble

When doing a lot of hand sewing you will find that you will soon puncture a hole in your middle finger where you push the needle through the fabric. Wearing a thimble is advisable – it will save a lot of discomfort later on.

Scissors

For accurate and neat work, a large pair of good quality, long-bladed, bent-handled scissors in the very finest condition is absolutely essential. They can be expensive but it is worth buying the best as they will last for years and will always be a pleasure to use. The handles should have a small hole for the thumb and a larger hole for the fingers, and should be bent to one side so that while you are cutting fabric, the blades will sit flat on the table. Choose a pair with the longest blades you can comfortably manage.

Special scissors with the hand position reversed are available for left-handed users. These should not be used for any other purpose than to cut fabric, or they will become spoilt. Do not allow anybody else in the house to use them. Keep a pair of general purpose kitchen scissors in your workbox for use when cutting paper or buckram, etc. to reduce the temptation to use your 'best' scissors for such purposes. A pair of small, short-bladed, sharp-pointed scissors for clipping fabric and trimming threads is another essential piece of equipment. All scissors should be sharpened regularly.

Rotary cutters have recently increased in popularity and are particularly good for cutting small pieces of fabric and bias strips, when they can be very accurate. They must only be used with special cutting mats made for the purpose. Again, they need to be kept sharp.

Threads

The colour of the thread should obviously be as close a match as possible to the colour of the fabric. If two colours make the choice difficult, it is better to choose the darker one because a single thread appears lighter when removed from the reel. Threads for soft furnishings should be of good quality and strong with a smooth finish. It is a false economy to buy cheap threads.

Where possible, it is best to match the composition of the thread to the fabric composition. The reason for this is simply because the fabric and thread cannot be treated differently once made up and the thread must be able to withstand the same washing and ironing temperatures as the fabric.

Tacking thread

Also known as basting thread, tacking thread is quite different to other sewing threads. It is loosely twisted cotton, which is very soft and unmercerized, and therefore breaks easily. This is very important for tacking threads, which are going to be pulled out. If they did not break so easily, there would be a risk of tearing the fabric. The thread is also quite hairy – another advantage – allowing it to grip the fabric and stay in place until ready to be removed. It is available in black and white.

Overlocking threads

These threads are specially designed for use with overlocking machines. To reduce bulk on an overlocked seam, they are finer than most sewing threads, but they must also be

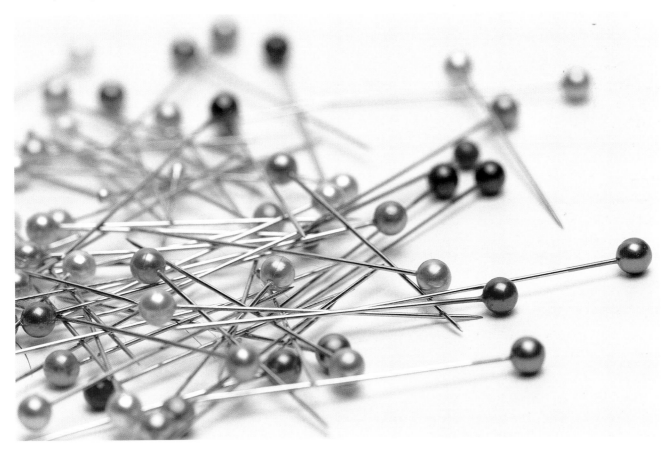

Long coloured headed pins are strong and easy to see. Always throw away blunt or rusty pins.

strong. As an overlocker uses vast amounts of thread, it is usually sold on huge cones with as much as 4,572 metres (5,000 yards) of thread on each cone. Special decorative threads are also available for use with an overlocker.

Sewing machines

If you already own a sewing machine, the chances are that it will be perfectly adequate for making soft furnishings as only the simplest machine is necessary. If you are about to buy a new one, consider a good second-hand model, otherwise one of the less complicated machines from a reputable manufacturer will be fine. Most of the machining involved in making soft furnishings is a simple straight stitch. Occasionally a zigzag is used for neatening.

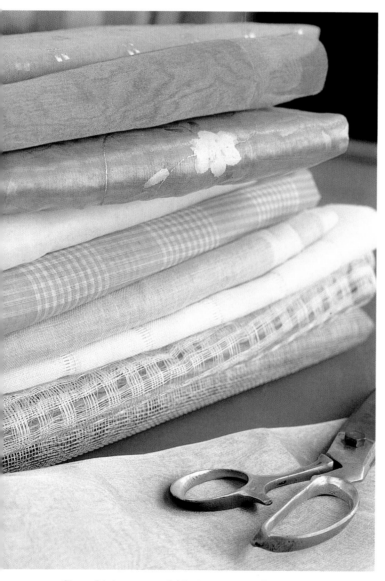

Sheer fabrics are available in a variety of textures.

Machine needles

Like hand sewing needles, machine needles need to be sharp or they will not only damage the fabric, but also put the machine's timing out, causing missed or badly formed stitches. If you consider how often a machine needle punctures the fabric in one seam, it is not surprising how soon it becomes blunt. Change the needle often. It is a good idea to do this for every project – this has the added advantage of making you think about choosing the correct needle for the task in hand.

Machine attachments

A walking foot is quite a useful additional extra for the machine. This is especially useful when matching patterns on seams as it helps prevent the top fabric from moving while you are machining. A piping foot is very useful if you intend to make a lot of piping. It straddles the cord, holding it in place and at the same time allows the machine to stitch close to the cord, giving a professional finish. If you don't have either of them, don't worry: they are helpful but not essential. A zipper foot, usually supplied with the machine, can be used for piping.

Overlocker

If you already own an overlocker, it can be useful for making soft furnishings but it is not essential.

Other equipment

A large table

This is perhaps the most awkward piece of equipment for the amateur home furnisher. When making curtains (drapes) or blinds (shades), it is essential that the full length of the fabric is placed flat to ensure accuracy. The floor is not ideal – particularly if it is carpeted – because you need to be able to slide the fabric. Instead, a good compromise is to buy a large piece of board to put over a table, which can be stored away when not in use. Chipboard would be adequate for this, if it is covered with heavy polythene or plastic to give it a smooth surface. If you are making a lot of curtains, it is essential that your table is the correct height, or else your back will soon suffer. It is possible to buy a large table, especially made as a sewing table, which is a good height and has flaps, that can be folded away when not in use.

Weights

A curtain placed on the table should be allowed to slip about easily, but it must also be restrained. Some kind of heavyweights are necessary for this purpose. There are lots of possibilities: an old flat iron covered with fabric is ideal, or a brick which has been padded and covered will do the job. Alternatively, you can use clips to hold the fabric to the table.

Pattern paper

For some projects you will need paper to make patterns or templates. Dressmakers' pattern cutting paper is ideal for this purpose.

Beeswax

A useful addition to the work basket. Thread can be strengthened by pulling it through the wax. Waxed thread is also less likely to knot.

Selecting a style

It can be very daunting to be faced with an empty room and to have to choose all the fabrics and furniture. Often your choice is restricted by existing carpets or furniture, but where do you start if you have carte blanche? The first thing to take into consideration is the kind of house: the period in which it was built, the size of the windows, doors, rooms, etc. Grand windows, doors and fireplaces cannot be ignored. On the contrary, they should be turned into features. If the house has large rooms with long windows with a very elegant feel, the fabrics chosen should reflect this. Brocades, silks, velvets and large patterned chintzes all look good in this situation. In contrast, a Tudor beamed cottage asks for smaller prints and cottage style fabrics. Some houses do not inflict their personality so strongly, however, and will absorb any style.

With increased travel and exposure to other cultures on television and in films, many international styles have become popular. The use of draped muslin reflects the mosquito nets of colonial style; Provençal prints introduce the bright colours of the south of France. You may prefer the crisp clean lines of Scandinavian countries, or in complete contrast, the rich crimsons and golds of the East. If you are unsure, seek inspiration in magazines and specialist shops, where the staff are usually very helpful and well-informed. Bring home fabric samples first to see how they look in your rooms. If necessary, buy just 10cm (4in). Colours often change in different lights and at various times of day. Live with these samples for a few days before making your final choice.

Finally, have faith in your choice. Your personality should shine through your rooms. It is always easier to admire somebody else's style and to copy it, but you won't really feel happy. Have what you like – you have to live with it!

Choosing fabric

Colour

Fabric colours can be divided into cold and warm shades, the cold ones being at the blue end of the spectrum, the warm ones at the red end. If your aim is to make a north-easterly room seem warm and cosy, it would be advisable to use warm colours and to avoid chilly blues. On the other hand, blues and whites would give a welcome coolness to a room in a hot climate.

Colours can be used to play another decorating trick, or optical illusion. Warm colours come towards you, while cooler colours recede. This means that an interior decorated in warm shades will seem smaller than when cool colours are used in the same room. Also, the lighter the colour used, the more it recedes and the darker the shade, the more it appears to come forward. Using this concept, we can deceive the eye and create a sense of space in small rooms, if we wish, by using light, cool colours. We can also appear to alter the shape of a room, e.g. if we have a long narrow room with a window at one end, by using warm coloured curtains the room will be foreshortened, making it seem squarer.

When choosing colours, consider all the practicalities. Light colours, particularly on fixed covers which cannot be removed for washing, soil more easily than dark and would not be practical if you have pets or children. Loose covers can be removed for washing. Dark colours may fade if they are near a south-facing window and subjected to a lot of sunshine. Bear in mind, too, that colours do go in and out of fashion and can become dated. If you want to avoid this, stick to more classical shades.

Plain or patterned?

After colour, pattern should be your next consideration. Patterns add a great deal of interest and personality to a

Metal hooks with sharp points are used to hang curtains with handmade headings.

room. Because there are so many beautiful patterns on the market, the choice can be confusing. Large patterns are best restricted to large rooms and to projects where the pattern is not going to be cut too much. Otherwise, the result will seem bitty and the overall effect will be lost and wasted. Large patterns need plenty of space to show off their glory. Similarly, small patterns look best in small areas. A small pattern repeated over and over again in a very large area can become tedious. Large patterns are generally less economical than smaller ones as a lot of fabric is sometimes wasted in trying to match the design.

The most economical fabric to use for soft furnishings is a plain colour with a plain weave since no pattern matching is necessary. Viewed from a distance, some tiny

Sew-on hooks for handmade curtain headings.

patterned fabrics can look like plainer ones with an interesting texture. Plain fabrics are generally less busy than patterned and more calming. The effect is simpler and more tailored. Of course there is no reason why a mixture of plain and patterned fabrics should not be used. In fact, this probably is the case in the majority of colour schemes, where the patterned fabric gives interest and the plain acts as a foil to it. Indeed, many of the leading fabric companies have created a whole range of complementary plains and patterns to make the choice much easier. A striped or checked fabric is a very useful go-between when using patterned and plain fabrics as it softens the contrast. On their own, checked and striped fabrics create a special look.

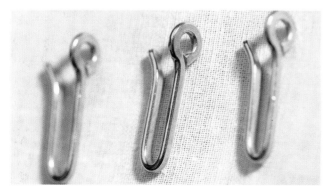

Detail of sew-on hooks.

Many plain fabrics, such as brocade and dobby weaves, have woven designs. The weaves break up the plainness of the fabric and make them more interesting. Fabric texture is also important. Shiny fabrics reflect light and sometimes appear cold and rather formal, whereas matt surfaces absorb light and seem warmer and more informal. On the other hand, they can sometimes appear dull and lifeless.

Other considerations

Cloth handle

Another important aspect to keep in mind when choosing fabric is the handle of the cloth. If a lot of seams are to be used the thickness has to be taken into account, even more so if piping is to be included in the seams – for instance in loose covers. Fabric must drape easily if it is to be used for swags, which should hang softly. To check this, hold the fabric up by its corner and see how it hangs across the bias grain. Study the label to see whether it needs to be washed or dry-cleaned. Check for creasing by crumpling a piece of fabric in your hand, releasing it and seeing if the creases fall out. Loose covers can look very untidy if made from material which creases badly.

Safety first

Legislation concerning flame resistance in fabrics changes all the time and varies from country to country. If in doubt, check the latest legislation before you make your selection. Fabrics used for covering furniture should be flame-retardant. This information should be stated clearly on the label. If your choice of fabric is not already treated, it is possible to have this done professionally.

Decorating fabric

One of the most important considerations when you are choosing fabric must be how much you can afford. When this is not an issue, life is easier but for those on a limited budget, all is not lost. The sales are a good hunting ground for reduced price fabrics, but watch out for sub-standard goods. Some very cheap fabrics can be used with exciting effects. Calico is a lovely, natural coloured, all-cotton fabric which can be used as it is, or it may be dyed very easily and effectively to the colour of your choice. For the more adventurous, tie-dyeing and batik give interesting results. Fabric can also be printed, painted or stencilled. Muslin is another cheap, all-cotton fabric, which can be treated in a similar way. The results are

very individual. Pillow ticking is a very hardwearing strong fabric which can look very smart. All you need is a bit of imagination.

Fabric customization need not be restricted to those on a budget. More expensive fabrics may be dyed or printed. Embroidery, patchwork, braids, cords and fringing all add interest to fabrics and can change their look dramatically.

A simple cheap white muslin tab top curtain.

Here, the same curtain is tie-dyed.

Special equipment for specific projects

Curtain weights

Curtain weights are made of lead. They are usually round and come in different sizes. They are inserted in the hems of curtains in each corner at at each seam. Their purpose is to pull down the curtain to counteract the tension on the seam and on the sides. The longer and heavier the curtain, the heavier the weights will need to be. They can be doubled up, if necessary.

Another type of curtain weight is made like a string of beads and is sold by the metre (yard). It is usually used to weigh down net or sheer curtains.

Both of the above are readily available in curtain fabric shops or departments.

Curtain hooks

Different hooks are needed for different heading tapes. Metal hooks with a sharp point are used for handmade pinch pleats and goblet headings. There are special plastic and metal hooks for machine tape heading and there are sew-on hooks which are also used for handmade headings.

Curtain poles & tracks

There are many types of poles and tracks available now. Poles come in different types of wood, metal and plastic, in different diameters and lengths. There are various tracks on the market, some are very strong and designed to support really heavy curtains, while others are flexible and good for windows with curves. You really need to seek advice when you are buying them.

Buckram

Buckram is a stiffened canvas. Two main types are used in soft furnishings: one type is used for stiffening hand-made curtain headings. This type is white and comes in different widths, the 12.5cm (5in) one being the most common. The other type of buckram is stiffened hessian and brown in colour. It is called pelmet buckram and used to stiffen pelmets and tiebacks.

Interlinings

Interlinings are used in curtains to add warmth and a look and feel of luxury. They are placed between the lining and the top fabric. The interlinings most commonly used are domette (synthetic) and bump (cotton).

Two types of buckram: piping cord and blackout lining.

Dressing windows

Measuring up for curtains

For greater accuracy, use a steel or wooden ruler, rather than a cloth tape measure.

Curtain widths

Measure the length of the curtain track, not the window. This might be longer than the window to allow the curtain to be drawn back beyond the window. If there is an overlap, add this measurement to the track.

Curtain lengths

This is the total length of the finished curtain. You must decide where the top of the curtain will be. This can be at the top of the track so that the track is covered when the curtain is closed, or if a decorative pole is used it might be just underneath this.

You must then decide where the lower edge of the curtain will fall. This could be on the sill, just below the sill, between the sill and the floor, draping onto the floor or longer than floor length so the curtain 'puddles' onto the floor. If the curtain is floor length, allow 1cm (⅜in) to clear the floor.

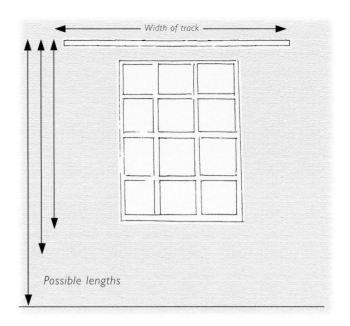

Possible lengths

Width of track

Estimating fabric quantities

Widths

Most furnishing fabrics are either 122cm (48in), 137cm (54in) or 150cm (60in) wide. The amount of fullness is a personal choice, but also depends on the heading used. It can be as little as one or one and a half times the width for a minimalistic look, or as much as three times for a very full look. For pencil pleats and pinch pleats the recommended amount is between two and a quarter to two and a half times the width.

Having measured the width of the track, multiply the measurement by the required fullness and divide the total by the fabric width. Round the figure up to the nearest width. This might be an odd number, but this is all right. (You can split a width and have a half width added to each curtain.) You now know the number of widths needed. Now you must work out the length of each width. For plain fabric, this is the required finished length plus the hem allowance of 15cm (6in), plus the top turning for the heading, or 5cm (2in) for commercial tape and 15cm (6in) for handheaded pinch pleats.

If there is a pattern which has to be matched, you might have to buy an extra pattern repeat for every width after the first one. With some pattern repeats, this can be quite expensive. You might wish at this stage to alter the length of the curtain to be more economical. Remember, though, that the surplus need not be wasted. It can be used for cushions (pillows), tiebacks, bows or valances, etc.

These hooks clip onto the curtain so there is no need for any sewing.

Simple door curtain

Door curtains keep out draughts, so saving on heating bills and they also give a cosy look to a room. A very effective curtain can be made by taking a length of fabric and simply finishing off the edges and adding a fringe. The chenille fabric used here looks good on both sides, so can be folded over without being lined.

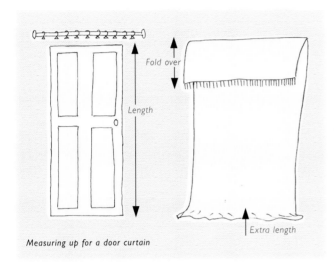

Measuring up for a door curtain

Materials & equipment
- fabric (see Measuring up, page 18 and above)
- fringe (the width of the curtain)
- curtain pole with rings and clips (see below)

Suitable fabrics
If your curtain is used to keep out draughts, you will probably want a heavy warm fabric for a cosy look. Chenille is ideal for this, but a heavy woollen tartan or tweed would look stunning. However, if warmth is not your objective and the purpose of your curtain is only to cover a glass or unsightly door, then any cotton or linen fabric would be fine.

Fringes
Fringes are wonderful. They can transform a simple curtain, cushion or throw into a luxurious item. There is a wealth of exciting fringes in the shops, in all colours, thicknesses and lengths. Some of the more complicated designs can be very expensive.

This cosy door curtain is made from chenille.

Pole
This particular door curtain hangs from a pole with rings and clips which grab the top of the curtain like miniature jaws. The rails and clips can be found at most DIY (home improvement) stores.

Method
1 Turn a hem around all sides of the fabric and handstitch or machine in place. Fold over 46cm (18in) of the fabric at the top. Stitch the fringe in place along the edge.
2 Attach clips and hang.

Fringes add a touch of luxury to cushions and curtains.

PROJECT 2

Sheer curtain
with simple slot heading

Sheer curtains are made of fine translucent fabric, such as net or muslin, silks, cotton or synthetics. They are usually kept drawn all the time to give extra privacy without blocking out too much light. Conventional curtains may be hung in front and opened and closed as usual. Traditionally, sheers have been made of cream or white fabric, but some beautiful coloured fabrics are now on the market, which give extra interest to a room. Sheer fabrics can also be used as curtains in their own right. When curtains are not strictly necessary, throwover drapes or dress curtains make particularly effective window frames. Sheer fabrics lend themselves perfectly to the minimalist look.

Sheers are not lined and they can either be weighted at the bottom to keep them under control, or allowed to float freely. They look better with plenty of fullness. Some fabrics are extra wide to avoid too many ugly seams, which will be seen through the fine fabric. If the widths need to be joined, use a run and fell seam, which looks neat on both sides and is completely flat.

Suitable fabrics
Any fine floaty fabric. It could be made of cotton, silk or synthetic fibres.

Hanging arrangements
Sheer curtains can have a variety of headings and may be hung from conventional rails or poles. In this project, however, a very simple slot heading, through which a pole is threaded, is used. The slot can be varied in size to accommodate different diameter poles.

Measuring up
To work out the amount of fabric needed, measure from under the pole to the required length. Add 10cm (4in) for the hem and 34cm (13½in) for the slot and heading. The heading will be 7.5cm (3in) and the slot will be 8.7cm (3½in). This slot will accommodate a pole up to 2.5cm (1in) diameter.

Adjust these measurements to fit your own pole and preferred height of heading.

A simple slot heading.

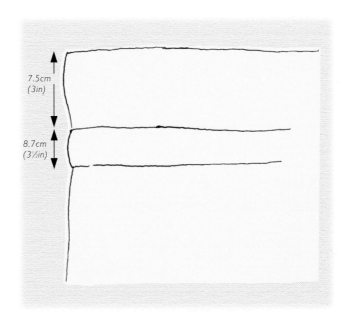

7.5cm (3in)

8.7cm (3½in)

Width: For a very full curtain, you will need two-and-a-half or three times the width of the pole, but for a simpler effect, one-and-a-half times would be enough.

Materials & equipment

- sheer curtain fabric (see Measuring up, page 20)
- T-square
- bead weights (optional)
- curtain pole (to hang, thread this through the top of the sheers)

Method

1 To straighten out the fabric, lay the bottom edge out on the table so that the selvedge lies exactly on the side edge of the table. Allow a little of the cut edge to hang over the end of the table and run a piece of tailor's chalk along the fabric where it hangs over the edge of the table, then cut along this line.

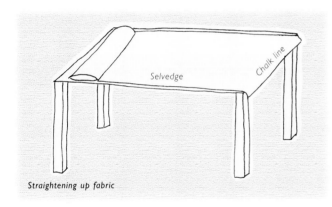

Straightening up fabric

2 Measure up the other lengths needed and mark across the fabric with chalk and a T-square. Cut across the line. Join the lengths, if necessary, using a run and fell seam. Turn in the sides with a narrow double hem. Machine or hem in place.

3 Press up a double 5cm (2in) hem at the bottom of the curtain. If a weighted hem is required, take a length of bead weights and stitch into the fold of the hem by hand. Refold the hem and slip stitch in place.

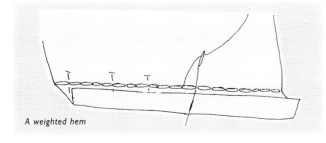

A weighted hem

4 With the curtain flat on the table, measure up the finished length from the hem using a metre rule or a yardstick. Mark the length with pins. Replace the pins with a line of tacking (basting). Turn over the top along the line of tacking stitches and tack again along the folded edge. Turn under the raw edge and pin down. Tack in place and machine along this bottom edge.

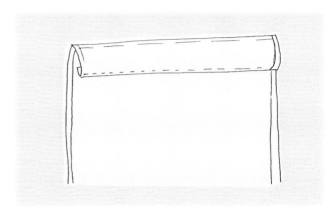

5 Machine again 8.7cm (3½in) above the first row to form a casing. Remove all tackings and press.

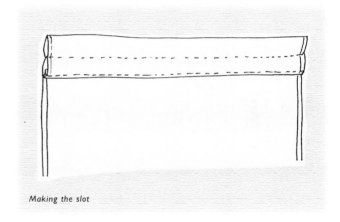

Making the slot

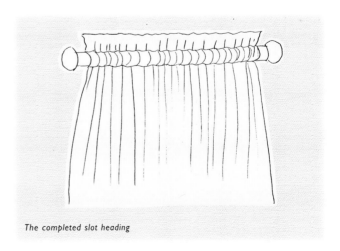

The completed slot heading

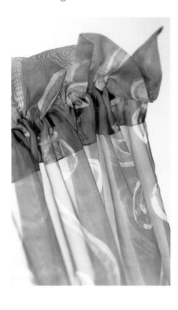

6 Thread the rod through the casing and arrange the gathers evenly. The curtain is now ready for hanging (left). Different effects can be achieved by varying the depth of the heading above the rod and also the width of the casing and size of rod.

TO ADD TAPE TO SHEER CURTAINS ...

• **Trim off the excess fabric leaving 2.5cm (1in) turned over.**

• **Pin, tack (baste) and machine the heading tape in position about 6mm (¼in) from the top. Turn in the cut ends of the tape. When machining the heading tape, machine both rows in the same direction.**

• **Machine down the ends of the tape being careful not to catch the cords. Remove all the tackings and press. To fit, pull up the gathers. Insert plastic hooks and hang.**

Neutral coloured sheer with heading tape.

PROJECT 3

Unlined tab top curtains

These attractive headed curtains (drapes) have become very popular recently. They fit in well with the simpler décor which is fashionable; they are also easy to make and look very effective. Tab top curtains do not pull back very neatly as the tabs bunch up on themselves. They can be left drawn at the top and opened and tied back with tiebacks. Therefore, they are better when they are not too full. As they do not use a great deal of fabric, they are relatively cheap to make.

Suitable fabrics

Most furnishing fabrics would be suitable for tab top curtains. There is no reason why they shouldn't be made of heavy fabric or the finest muslin. Wools, silks, cotton, linen or synthetics can be used.

Hanging arrangements

Tab top curtains need to hang from a pole which is threaded through the tabs. This can be made of wood, iron, brass or steel. As the tabs act as hangers, there is no need for any kind of rings or hooks.

Measuring up

To keep this project simple, only one width of fabric is used in each curtain. As most curtain fabric is 122 or 137cm (48 or 54in) wide, these curtains will fit windows up to 178cm (70in) wide. If you need to make them wider, you will need to join widths.

Measure the length from the top of the pole to the desired length. Take away 10cm (4in) for the length of the tabs. Add 16.5cm (6½in) for the hem and seam allowance. Add 30cm (12in) for the tabs and facings. This represents the amount of fabric you will need for one curtain.

Materials & equipment
- curtain fabric
- pole for hanging

Method
1 First, cut a strip of fabric 23cm (9in) wide across the width of the fabric. Divide this equally into seven or eight strips depending on the width of the fabric. The strips should be about 18 or 20cm (7 or 8in) wide.

Tab top curtains are stylish and easy to make.

Then cut another strip 7.5cm (3in) wide across the width of the fabric. This is for the facing. Fold the strips for the tabs in half lengthways with right sides inside and machine together along the length with 1.3cm (½in) seam allowance (1.3cm/½in from the raw edges). Press, turn the strip to the right side and press.

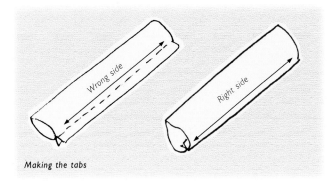

Making the tabs

2 Turn a narrow hem down each side of the curtain. Machine in place, then press.

3 Make a 7.5cm (3in) double hem along the bottom of the curtain and machine in place. Oversew the sides of the hem by hand.

4 Fold the tabs in half so that the raw edges are together. Pin to hold in place. Position one tab at each end of the top of the curtain and the others at equal distances in between. Pin and tack (baste) them to the right side of the curtain so that the raw edges of the tabs line up with the raw curtain edge.

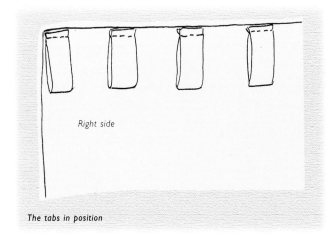

The tabs in position

5 Now take the facing and lay it on top of the tabs with the right side down (touching the tabs) and with the raw edge matching up with the raw edge of the top of the curtain. Pin, tack and machine in position using a 1.3cm (½in) seam allowance.

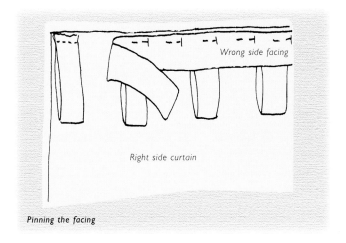

Pinning the facing

6 Press. Now fold the facing over to the back of the curtain. Turn under 1.3cm (½in) along the long edge and pin, tack and machine to the curtain.

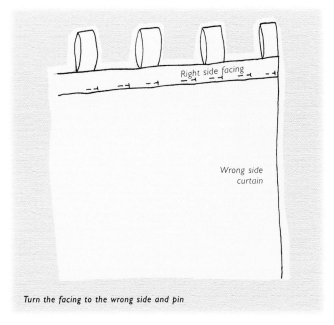

Turn the facing to the wrong side and pin

7 Tuck in the edges and oversew by hand. Press the finished curtains, thread the rod through the tabs. Hang.

DECORATING IDEAS

• **Add interesting buttons to the base of your tabs. These could be wooden or horn, or you could cover your own buttons with self or contrasting fabric.**

• **Make the tabs of a contrasting colour and add a matching tieback.**

This tab top curtain in natural coloured fabric adds a touch of cool elegance to any room.

Linings

In general, like clothes, curtains (drapes) hang better if they are lined. More light is blocked out and the lining acts as a protection against strong sunlight, which fades and rots fabric through time. It is far cheaper to renew the lining than the whole curtain later on. Lined curtains are also warmer.

Special curtain lining is usually used. It is made from cotton sateen and is available in shades of white cream and ecru as well as a range of colours. Natural shades are usually preferred as colours tend to fade, but used imaginatively, coloured lining can give some lovely effects, e.g. lining natural coloured curtains with a deep coral gives a warm glow to the fabric. But you don't have to stick to special curtain lining material: contrasting prints may also be used to great effect. Striped fabric lining flowered curtains can also look very smart.

Curtain lining is available in 122cm (48in) and 137cm (54in) widths. Make sure you buy the same width lining as the top fabric.

A neutral lining works well with checks.

Special linings

There are some additional linings available which deserve a mention. Blackout lining, which surprisingly is white in colour, is very effective in blocking out the light completely. It is therefore suitable for a child's room, or for a room next to a street light. Millium lining is silver in colour and designed to give extra warmth.

Here, the lining forms part of the tail design.

Add warmth to your rooms with interlined curtains.

Interlining

It is not surprising that interlined curtains have become so popular. They have such a luxurious look and feel, and are also very warm and cosy. It is very expensive to have interlined curtains made, so you can save yourself a lot of money by making your own (pages 32–5). Several different interlinings are available: some are made from cotton while others are synthetic. Again, they are available in two widths.

Some curtains are better left unlined. The delicate floaty effect of sheer fabrics is sometimes lost if they are lined. Small gingham checks at a cottage window may lose their attractive simplicity if they are lined. The recent trend towards more simplistic window treatments tends to favour the unlined look.

Estimating quantities

Make sure the lining is the same width as the curtain fabric. Measure up for lining in the same way as for measuring plain fabric for curtains (page 18). You will need 2.5cm (1in) less on each width.

PROJECT 4

Lined curtains with pencil pleat heading

From unlined curtains with simple headings, we now move on to lined curtains with a machined heading.

Machined headings

Years ago all pleated and gathered headings had to be made by hand. Now life is much simpler and we can buy several types of heading tape which do the pleating for us. To form the pleats, these tapes are simply machined to the top of the curtain and the cord pulled up to the desired length. The hooks are removed for cleaning and the cords released so that the curtain lies flat again.

One of the most popular types of tape is pencil pleating tape which is available in more than one width. A very lightweight tape is especially suitable for lightweight fabrics.

Suitable fabrics

Most fabrics are suitable for machine headings although finer and medium weight fabrics pleat up better than thicker ones. Cottons, linens and silks will work well.

Hanging arrangements

These curtains hang from a rail by hooks which are slotted into pockets on the tape. On pencil pleating tape there are three choices of position for the rings. If the hooks are placed in the top row of the pockets, the curtain will hang below the rail. When placed in the bottom row, the rail will be hidden when the curtains are closed. The hooks then hang from rings on a curtain rail or pole. There is a wide range of choice of rails and poles available. Seek advice on the suitability and strength of the rail or pole before you buy.

Measuring up

See general notes, pages 18 and 26.

Materials & equipment

- fabric (see Measuring up, page 18)]
- lining that is the same width as the fabric (see Measuring up, page 26)
- heading tape (enough for each curtain width)
- curtain weights (one for each seam and one for each corner)
- 4 plastic cord tidies
- plastic hooks

Heading tape for pencil pleats.

Preparation

Prepare the fabric by laying it out on the table with the selvedge exactly along the length of the table. The cut edge of the fabric should sit exactly parallel to the end of the table. If not, allow a little of the fabric to hang over the end of the table. Take a piece of tailor's chalk and run it along the fabric where it falls over the edge of the table. Cut along the chalk line. Repeat with the lining.

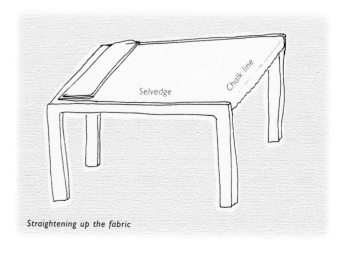

Straightening up the fabric

Cutting out

Lining

Measure the lengths of lining and mark with a pin (tack). Using a T-square and tailor's chalk, draw a line across the lining and cut across this line.

Top fabric

If using plain fabric, measure and cut the lengths in the same way as for the lining but if using patterned fabric, the patterns must match so, starting from the bottom, measure the required length and mark with a pin. The bottom edge of the next drop must start at the same place on the pattern as the first, so find the first point in the pattern after the pin and mark that. Measure out all the lengths in this way before you cut. At this stage it is a good idea to recheck. Once satisfied, using a T-square, draw across the fabric to mark the cutting lines. Cut the lengths.

Method

1 The lead curtain weights should be covered to make sure that they do not mark the fabric. To do this, take a piece of scrap lining. Wrap the fabric over the weight and make a small running stitch around the weight.

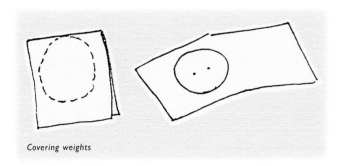

Covering weights

2 Join the lengths of lining together by machine and press the seams open. Fold up a double 7.5cm (3in) hem on the lining and machine in place. Pin the lengths of top fabric together carefully matching the patterns on the fabric. Once made up, the seam should be almost invisible. Machine the lengths together and press the seams open.

3 Place one curtain on the table wrong side up. Turn under a single 3.8cm (1½in) hem down both sides. Press in place. Turn up a double 7.5cm (3in) hem along the bottom of the curtain and press in place. Mitre the corners by unfolding the sides of the fabric and one fold of the hem.

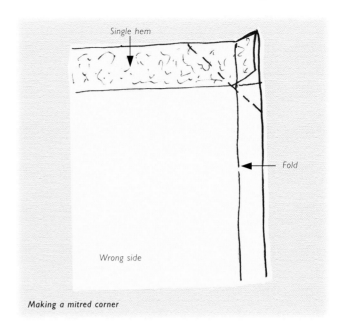

Making a mitred corner

4 Now make a diagonal fold across the corner exactly through the point where the hem and side folds meet. Line up the fold lines on the corner with those on the curtain.

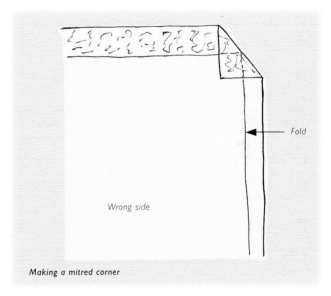

Making a mitred corner

Pencil-pleated curtain.

5 Fold the second fold of the hem and the side fold back in place so that the diagonal folds of the mitre butt together.

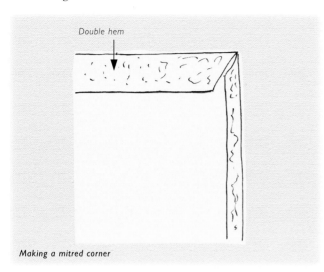

Making a mitred corner

6 Slip a covered weight into the corner under the mitre. Do a few stitches to attach it securely to the curtain, making sure that the bottom of the weight sits on the bottom edge of the curtain. Stitch the mitre together with ladder stitch (page 107).

Ladder stitch mitre

Make sure the bottom corner of the lining lies exactly on the mitre.

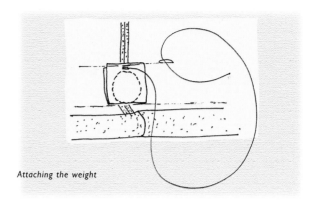

Attaching the weight

7 Position a covered weight inside the hem so that the bottom edge of the weight touches the bottom edge fold of the curtain. Stitch securely in place.

8 Pin the side folds and the bottom hem back in position and stitch in place. Serge stitch the sides and slip hem the bottom. Join the lining lengths if necessary. Turn up a double 7.5cm (3in) hem at the bottom edge and machine in place.

9 Lay the curtain on the table wrong side up and smooth out any wrinkles. Now lay the lining on top right side up so that wrong sides of both fabrics are together. Adjust the lining so that the bottom edge is about 2.5cm (1in) above the bottom edge of the curtain. Make sure that the hems are parallel and the seams line up. Smooth out.

10 The lining must be attached to the fabric so that both the fabrics hang as one. This is done with a locking stitch. Carefully peel back the lining halfway along its length. Make sure the other half of the curtain is undisturbed. Lock stitch down the fold of the lining onto the main fabric. These stitches show through to the front side of the curtain so must be quite small. Don't worry too much, though, as they will be lost in the folds of the curtain.

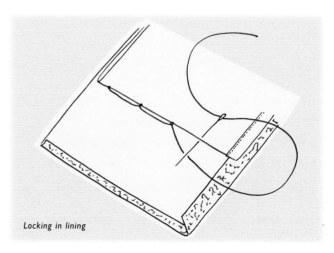

Locking in lining

Pencil-pleated heading.

11 Smooth the lining back in place and then repeat this process on every seam and on every half width. When the locking is completed, smooth the lining back in place and turn under the sides of the lining onto the curtain about 2.5cm (1in) from the folded edge of the curtain. Make sure the bottom corner of the lining lies exactly on the mitre. Slip stitch the lining in place along the sides and 5cm (2in) around the corner onto the bottom hem.

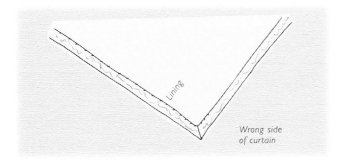

Lining

Wrong side
of curtain

12 Using a metre rule or wooden yardstick, measure the finished length of the curtain from the hem to the top. Mark the position with a pin. Do this at regular intervals across the width of the curtain. Using a long ruler, chalk a line joining the pins. Replace the pins with a row of tacking (basting) stitches, stitching through both fabrics.

13 Fold over the top edge of the curtain along this tacked line and tack the folded edge down. Tack and machine the heading tape in position about 6mm (¼in) below the top. It is preferable to machine these two rows in the same direction to avoid skewing the top of the curtain. Fold in the cut ends and stitch down, making sure not to catch in the gathering threads.

14 Press the curtain well and pull up the gathering threads to the required length. Wrap the spare threads around the cord tidy. Put the hooks in the pockets on the tape and hang. If the curtain has a half width, the half width should be hung at the outside edge. For dressing instructions, see Interlined Curtains, pages 32–7).

Wrong side of the pencil pleats with the heading tape.

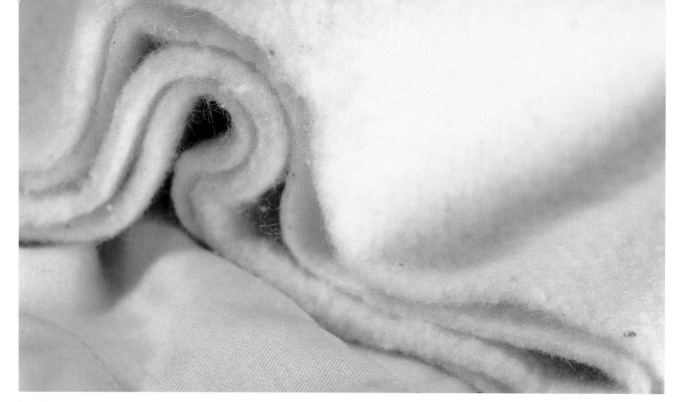

Interlining curtains gives a luxurious effect as well as providing added insulation.

PROJECT 5

Interlined curtains
with handmade heading

For a luxurious effect, try interlined curtains. They will make even the cheapest fabric look good. Apart from aesthetics, there are several practical advantages, too. Interlined curtains provide added insulation – they block out draughts and help cut out noise. Being much thicker than most other curtains, they also cut out more light. Although time consuming to make, they are well worth the extra effort.

Suitable fabrics

Most cotton, silk or linen fabrics are suitable for interlined curtains. Remember that interlined curtains are quite thick when they are finished so it is better not to use too thick fabric to start with.

Materials & equipment

- curtain weights (one for each seam and one for each corner)
- fabric, see Measuring up, page 18
- lining, the same width as the fabric
- interlining, see Measuring up, page 26
- buckram, enough for the width of the curtains
- metal pins or sew-on hooks

Method

1 The lead curtain weights should be covered to make sure that they do not mark the fabric. To do this, take a piece of scrap lining. Wrap the fabric over the weight and make a small running stitch around the weight.

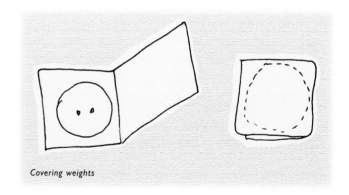

Covering weights

2 Prepare the fabric by laying it out on the table with the selvedge exactly along the table's length. The cut edge of the fabric should sit exactly parallel with the end of the table. If not, allow a little of the fabric to hang over the end. Take a piece of tailor's chalk and run it along the fabric where it falls over the edge of the table, then cut along the chalk line (see Lined Curtains, pages 28–31).

3 Measure the required length from this point and put in a pin. The bottom edge of the next drop must start at the same place on the pattern as the first. Find the first point in the pattern after the pin and mark it. Measure

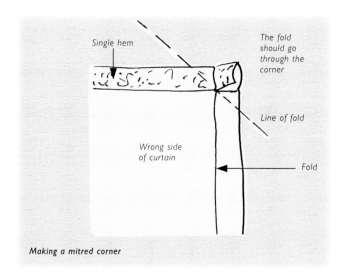

Making a mitred corner

out all the lengths in this way before you start to cut the fabric. At this point it is a good idea to recheck. Once satisfied, using a T-square, draw across the fabric to mark the cutting lines and cut out lengths of fabric.

4 Now cut out the lining and the interlining. Join the lining with conventional plain seams. The interlining is better joined flat so that it is not too bulky. Pin the lengths of top fabric together, carefully matching the patterns on the fabric. Once made up the seam should be almost invisible. Machine the lengths together and press the seams open.

5 Place one curtain on the table wrong side up. Turn under a single 3.8cm (1½in) hem down both sides and press in place. Turn up a double 7.5cm (3in) hem along the bottom of the curtain; press in place.

6 Mitre the corners by unfolding the sides of the fabric and one fold of the hem.Make a diagonal fold across the corner exactly through the point where the hem and side folds meet. Line up the fold lines on the corner with those on the curtain.
Fold the second fold of the hem and the side fold back

in place so the diagonal folds of the mitre butt together.

7 Open out the side folds and one hem fold. Lay the curtain wrong side up on the table. Smooth it out so there are no wrinkles. Lay the interlining over the curtain and smooth it out. There should be no wrinkles in either curtain or interlining. The edges of the interlining should line up with the sides of the curtain and the first hem fold.

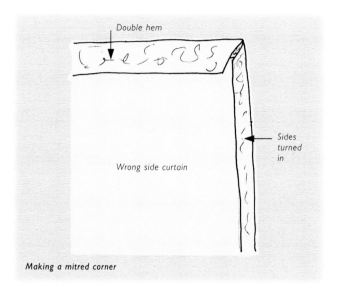

Making a mitred corner

8 The interlining must be attached to the fabric so that both fabrics hang as one. This is done with a locking stitch. Carefully peel back the interlining halfway along its length. Make sure the other half of the curtain is left undisturbed. Lock stitch down the fold of the interlining onto the main fabric. Smooth the interlining back into place and repeat this process on every seam and on every half width.

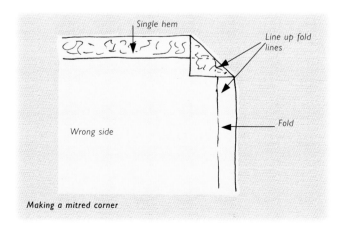

Making a mitred corner

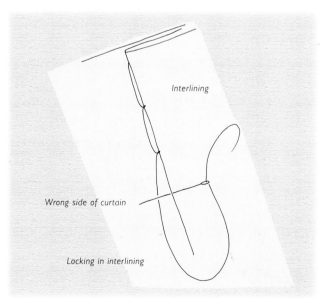

Locking in interlining

9 Turn back the interlining along the sides as far as the curtain fold. In the gulley formed by the fold, stitch the interlining to the curtain using small lock stitches about 5cm (2in) apart. Repeat on the other side and along the second fold of the hem. Trim away any excess interlining, if necessary. The edges of the interlining should not be visible when the sides and hem are refolded.

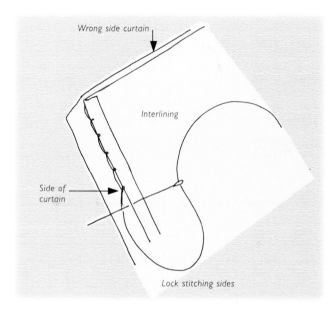

Wrong side curtain

Interlining

Side of curtain

Lock stitching sides

10 Slip a covered weight into the corner under the mitre. Do a few stitches to attach it securely to the curtain, making sure that the bottom of the weight sits on the bottom edge of the curtain. Position a covered weight on each seam inside the hem so that the bottom edge of the weight touches the bottom edge of the curtain fold. Stitch securely in place.

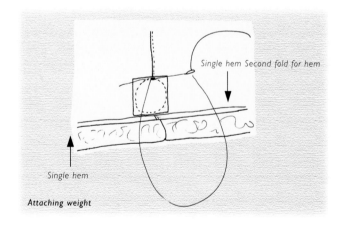

Single hem   Second fold for hem

Single hem

Attaching weight

Pin the side folds and the bottom hem back in position. Join the mitre with ladder stitch.

Join the mitre together with ladder stitch

Serge stitch the sides and slip hem the bottom.

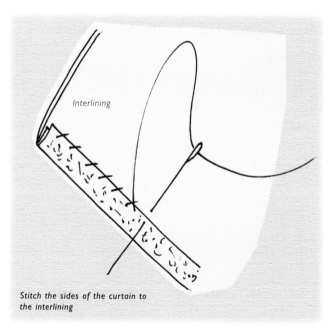

Interlining

Stitch the sides of the curtain to the interlining

11 Join the lining lengths, if necessary. Turn up a double 7.5cm (3in) hem at the bottom edge and machine in place.

12 The interlined curtain should still be flat on the table. Smooth out any wrinkles and lay the lining on top, right side up, so the wrong side of the lining faces the interlining. Adjust the lining so the bottom edge is about 2.5cm (1in) above the bottom edge of the cur-tain.Make sure the hems are parallel and the seams line up. Smooth out any wrinkles and lay the lining on top, right side up, so the wrong side of the lining faces the interlining. Adjust the lining so the bottom edge is about 2.5cm (1in) above the bottom edge of the curtain. Make sure the hems are parallel and the seams line up; smooth out.

13 The lining must now be locked to the interlining in the same way as the interlining was locked to the curtain by peeling back the lining and locking at every seam and every half width.

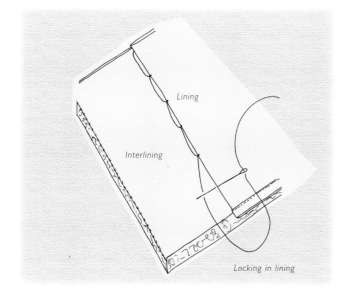

When the locking is completed, smooth the lining back in place and turn under the lining sides onto the curtain about 2.5cm (1in) from the folded edge of the curtain. Make sure the bottom corner of the lining lies exactly on the mitre. Slip stitch the lining in place along the sides and 5cm (2 in) around the corner at the bottom of the curtain.

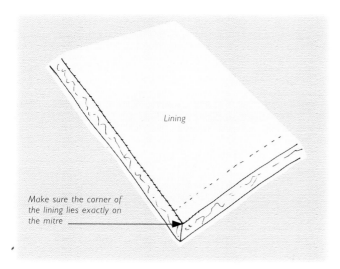

14 Using a metre rule or wooden yard stick, measure the finished curtain length from the lower edge to the top. Mark the position with a pin. Do this at regular intervals across the top of the curtain. Replace the pins with a row of tacking (basting) stitches, stitching through all the fabrics.

Place the top edge of the buckram along the line of tacking. Turn the curtain top over the buckram and under its lower edge. Pin in place. It is preferable for the fabric, lining and interlining to be taken over the buckram and tucked underneath, but in some cases this is too bulky. If so, cut away the interlining near the top of the curtain. Oversew the ends. Press the curtain well.

Measuring pinch pleats

Unlike commercial heading tapes, which can be pulled up to fit any size of window, handmade pinch pleats are made to fit a particular window and are stitched permanently in position. It is important, therefore, that they are measured accurately. You usually allow about two and a half times the width for the fullness of a pinch pleated heading.

Measuring pinch pleats is tricky. I have tried to give you a very simplified method here to get you started. Measure the width of the track. Add to this any overlap and return, if necessary. Now measure the width of the curtain (as it is at the stage when ready to do the pinch pleats). The difference between the two measurements is the amount available for the pleats. Each pleat should take about 12.5 or 15cm (5 or 6in) of fabric. The thicker the fabric, the more will be needed. Divide the available fabric for pleats by five. If the figure is a fraction, round it

Detail of pinch pleats from the wrong side.

down to a whole number. Now divide the available fabric by this number to work out how big the pleats should be. It does not matter if this is a fractional number. It should be between 12.5 and 15cm (5 and 6in). Thicker fabrics need more fabric for pleats (nearer 15cm/6in) so you might have to have less pleats to make each one bigger. There should be an equal number of gaps or spaces, so divide the track length by the number of pleats to make sure the gaps are a sensible size. They should be somewhere between 7.5 and 15cm (3 and 6in). Sometimes this does not work out and you need to recalculate and maybe add or take away one pleat.

The end gap or space allowance should be divided equally between the two ends. If you have a return on your curtain, the measurements must be adjusted so that the end gap or space is the same size as the return and the last pleat sits on the corner of the rail. It is a good idea to make a plan of pleats and spaces on a piece of paper to make sure they all add up before starting on your curtain.

Making pinch pleats

1 First, work out the required number of pleats and gaps (see above) and mark these with pins on the curtain.
2 Make the pleats by folding the top edge of the curtain wrong sides together until two pins marking a pleat meet. Make sure the top edges are lined up. Pin this pleat in position and machine exactly parallel to the folded edge of the pleat. You can mark this either by measuring and marking with tailor's chalk or make a cardboard template and use this as a guide. This has the added advantage of ensuring that all the pleats are exactly the same size. Machine all pleats.

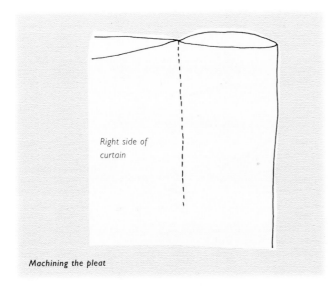

Machining the pleat

3 Take hold of each pleat between the finger and thumb at the fold edge and push it back to the machined edge. Two pleats should form at either side of the middle one.

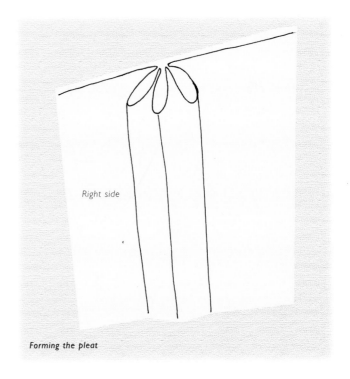

Forming the pleat

Stitch these in place by hand at the top and bottom edge of the pleat. If the curtains have a half width, the half width is always hung at the outside edge. Insert metal pins or sew-on metal hooks behind each pleat and at each end. The curtain is now ready to be hung.

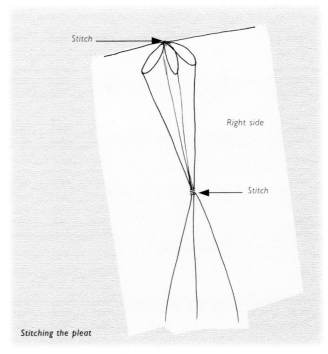

Stitching the pleat

Goblet pleats

These pleats look very sophisticated. They are particularly suited to large elegant windows. The disadvantage of them is that they do not draw back neatly and are usually left drawn at the top and the curtains held open with tiebacks.

Measuring up

This is exactly the same as for pinch pleats and the making up is the same up to the forming of the pleats. After machining, instead of forming the three pleats, all you have to do is gather up the base of the pleat and stitch in place by hand. Now 'stuff' the goblet with a rolled-up piece of curtain buckram. Put the pin hooks (or sew-on hooks) into the back of the pleats as for pinch pleats.

Dressing curtains

When the curtains are hung, they usually need coaxing to hang beautifully. Draw the curtains back and sort out the pleats at the heading. Now stroke down the folds until they hang correctly. Starting from the top, bind the curtains with strips of spare fabric or lining. Leave in place overnight and then release the bindings.

Goblet pleats.

Working with pattern

It is especially pleasing if you can make the pleats fit into the pattern on the fabric, but this is quite advanced and not strictly necessary.

It is especially pleasing if the pleats can be fitted into the pattern of the fabric.

PROJECT 6

Roman blind

Roman blinds (shades) require very little fabric and are therefore relatively cheap to make. They can either be used on their own to give a smart uncluttered look or you can hang them behind dress curtains, where they cut down on the amount of curtain fabric needed.

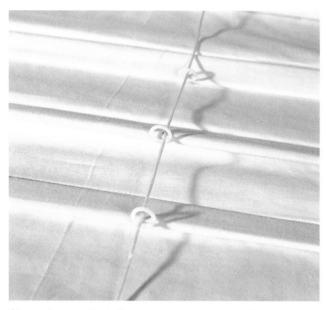

Choose Roman blinds for a clean, uncluttered look.

They are quite easy to make. The most difficult part is working out the positions of the folds and the batten slots. I have tried to make this as simple as possible.

Suitable fabrics

Fabrics for Roman blinds need to be closely woven and not too thick. Cotton and linen are ideal. Ordinary curtain lining is suitable for the backing but any other similar cotton would be fine.

Hanging arrangements

The blind needs a board to support it. This needs to be the same width as the blind and is fixed above the window with angle brackets.

Materials & equipment

- top fabric (see Suitable fabrics and Measuring up)
- lining (see below)
- wooden battens, 2.5cm x 3mm (1 x ⅛in)
- strong linen thread
- packet of small plastic or brass rings, about 1.3cm (½in) in diameter
- nylon cord (the amount depends on the size of blind)
- Velcro (enough for the width of the blind)
- board for fixing the blind (the same width as the blind)
- packet of screw eyes or china cord guides
- cleat (for wall-fixing)

Measuring up

Roman blinds are a little tricky to measure so I have tried to give a foolproof method to avoid mistakes. First, decide where the blind is going to be fitted, inside or outside the window recess. Measure the desired width and length.

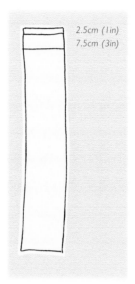

Top fabric

Add 10cm (4in) to the width and 7.5cm (3in) to the length for turnings. This is the measurement for the top fabric.

Lining

The slots for the blind are accommodated in the lining so extra fabric must be allowed for them. The easiest way to do this is to make a plan on paper. Take a strip of paper a few centimetres (inches) wide and the length of the finished blind plus 2.5cm (1in). Mark off the first 2.5cm (1in) by drawing a line across the paper. This represents the turning at the top of the blind. Now make another line 7.5cm (3in) below this. This 7.5cm (3in) allows for the board on which the blind hangs.

Divide the rest of the strip for the folds of the blind. The folds are usually between 15 and 20cm (6 and 8in). Divide the rest of the strip into an odd number of equal sized folds, each somewhere between 15 and 20cm (6 and 8in). Mark these divisions on the paper.

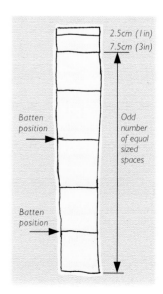

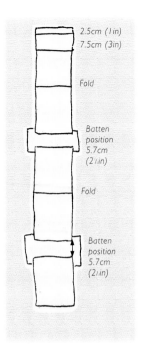

The battens will be positioned at every second fold marking. Try folding the paper to make sure you have done this correctly. Now cut across the paper at the positions of the battens. Make a gap of 5.7cm (2¼in) and insert pieces of paper behind the gaps. This strip represents the length of the lining to be cut. The width of the lining will be 5cm (2in) narrower than the top fabric.

Cutting out

Straighten up the fabric by laying it out on the table with the selvedges parallel to the sides of the table. Allow the fabric to fall over the end of the table slightly. Run tailor's chalk along the edge and cut along this line (see straightening fabric, page 28.

Making up

Top fabric

Turn in 5cm (2in) on both sides of the top fabric and press. Turn up a single 5cm (2in) hem on the bottom of the blind. Form mitres on the corners Press and serge stitch the sides and the hem, but leave the mitres open.

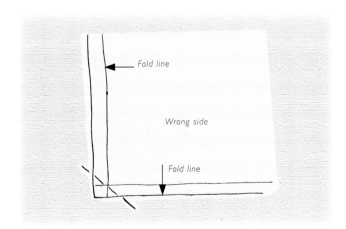

Lining

Turn under 2.5cm (1in) of the sides and the bottom of the lining. Tack (baste) and press in place. Using your paper pattern as a guide, mark the slot positions on the right

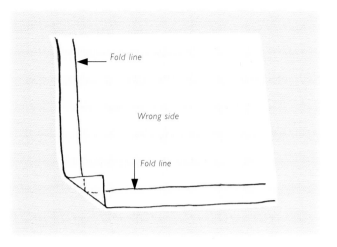

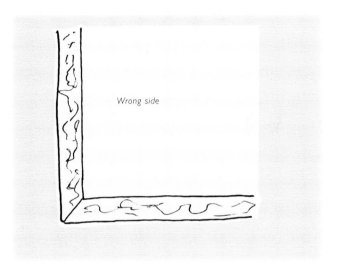

side with tailor's chalk (or a light sensitive pen) and a long ruler. Fold the lining to the wrong side so that the slot markings line up. Tack and machine along the lines.

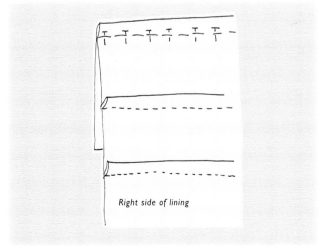

Working on a flat surface, spread out the top fabric wrong side up. Place the lining on top of the main fabric wrong sides together. The slots will be uppermost and the sides and the bottom of the lining should be 2.5cm (1in) inside the top fabric. Pin in place along the sides, the bottom and across the slots. Slip stitch the sides of the lining to the main fabric, keeping the ends of the slots free and open. Slip stitch the lining to the bottom of the blind.

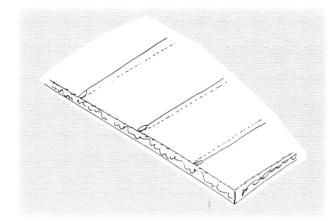

Tack the lining to the top fabric just under the slots and machine through both fabrics.

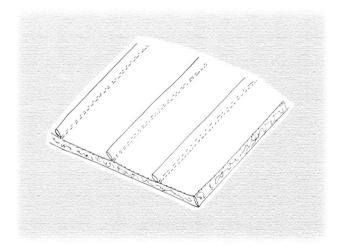

Measure the finished length from the hem at intervals and mark with pins. Tack along the pin line. Turn the fabric over on this line and tack along the fold. Trim any excess fabric to 1cm (½in). Pin and tack the Velcro in position. Machine along the top and bottom of it. Insert the battens into the slots and oversew the ends. Put one batten into the hem and stitch the mitres with ladder stitch. Sew rings onto the batten slots using strong linen thread.

The outside rings should be positioned about 5 or 7.5cm (2 or 3in) in from the outside edge and the other rings spaced equally between, no more than 38cm (15in) apart.

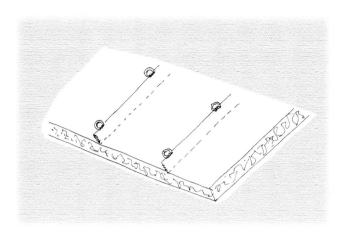

Attach the rough side of the Velcro to the edge of the board with staples or tacks. (It is possible now to buy self-adhesive Velcro but I still like the extra security of tacks or staples.) You then need to screw in the eyes or guides under the board to correspond with the rings on the blind.

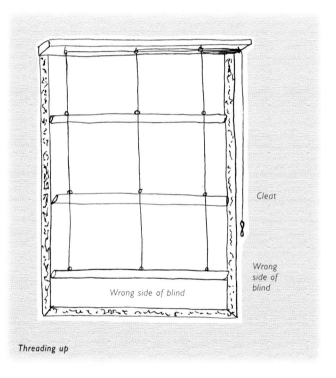

Cleat

Wrong side of blind

Wrong side of blind

Threading up

Threading up

Measure your lengths of cord. You need a separate length for each vertical row of rings. The blind is threaded up by attaching the separate cords to the bottom row of rings with a knot. These cords are threaded through the vertical line of rings above and then through the corresponding eye under the board. The cords are then threaded along the board through the other eyes to one side of the board. Plait the cord together at this point and take down to the cleat on the wall.

Window accessories

Simple throwover swag

Where curtains (drapes) are not strictly necessary, a throwover swagged curtain is an effective way of softening the lines of a window. Once in position, the swagged curtain is not moved. Similarly, a shorter version can be used above conventional curtains as a decorative swagged pelmet (valance).

Measuring up
Use a long length of string or ribbon and drape this over the pole allowing the required drape in the middle. Cut off the string at the required lengths.

Measure the string, add 5cm (2in) for hems and you have the length of fabric you need.

Method
The easiest way to achieve this effect is to throw a long piece of fabric over a pole and then arrange it. Hem the ends and sides of the fabric to neaten them. If the fabric has a definite right and wrong side, it will need to be cut and rejoined where it twists over the pole so that the right side is always visible.

Delicate beads are light enough not to distort this sheer swag.

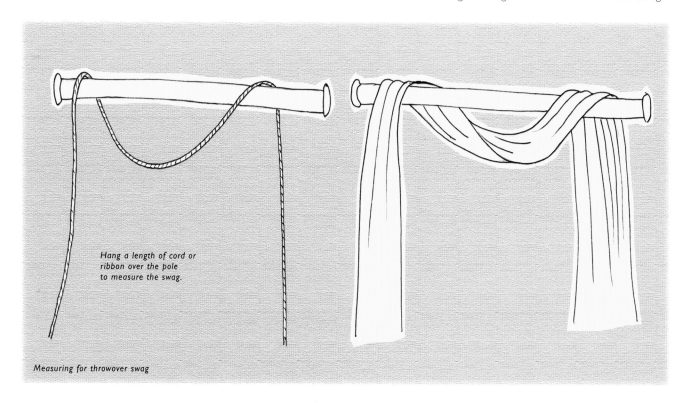

Hang a length of cord or ribbon over the pole to measure the swag.

Measuring for throwover swag

Light and airy, this throwover swag gives the room a feeling of tranquillity and elegance.

Stitch the Velcro on the top edge of the valance.

Pelmets and valances

Pelmets and valances are fixed across and above the top of a curtain (drape). Not only do they hide the rail and the curtain headings and any other untidy features at the top of the window, they can also be used to give an illusion of height. Often their purpose is solely decorative. When curtains are open, they provide added interest and without a pelmet, a window can sometimes look quite bare. As a valance or pelmet covers the top of a curtain, a simple heading on the curtain will suffice.

Pelmets are sometimes made of wood or hardboard, and simply painted, varnished or stencilled. They can also be covered with fabric. Pelmets give a more formal, rather tailored look. Valances are usually gathered or pleated, and are softer in appearance.

The depth of the pelmet or valance is a matter of taste. To make a window look taller, the pelmet or valance can be fixed slightly higher than the top of the window with the base just covering the top. This has the added advantage of cutting out the minimum of light. Normally pelmets and valances are between 15cm (6in) and 30cm (12in) high, but this is not a fixed rule. They can also be shaped so that the sides are longer than the middle.

Gathered valance

A gathered valance gives a softer, less formal look to a window than a stiff pelmet. It is very easy and satisfying to make.

Suitable fabrics
Any curtain fabric would be fine for a valance. Usually they are made in the same fabric as the curtains they hang over, but contrasting fabric could also be used.

Hanging arrangements
Like swags and tails, valances are attached to a special board with Velcro. Alternatively, special rails can be bought, in which case hooks would be used for hanging.

Measuring up

Top fabric
Measure the width of the board or rail including any return. You will need two and a half to three times this length for the width of your valance. Divide this measurement by the width of the fabric to discover how many widths of fabric you need. Round the figure up or down to get a whole number. For pencil-pleated valances it is usually better to err on the generous side.

Measure the desired length of your valance and add 6cm (2½in) for turnings.

Multiply this length by the number of widths. You now have the amount of fabric needed if you are using plain fabric. Remember to take the pattern repeat into consideration for patterned fabric.

Lining
You will need the same number of widths as for the top fabric, but the length of each width will be the finished length plus 1.3cm (½in).

Making up
1 First, cut out the fabric and lining and join the widths.
2 Lay the fabric on the table right side up and lay the lining on top, wrong side up. Pin together at the bottom edge. Machine using a 1.3cm (½in) seam allowance.

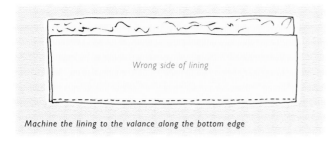

Machine the lining to the valance along the bottom edge

3 Press the seam up towards the lining. Now rearrange the lining so that the top edge of the lining and the top fabric are even. Pin, tack (baste) and machine the ends. Press.

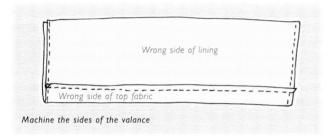

Machine the sides of the valance

4 Turn the valance to the right side. Match up the top edges again and tack them together. Now carefully press the bottom edge. The top fabric will be wrapped around to the back.

5 Turn over 2.5cm (1in) of the raw edges at the top of the valance. Pin and tack. Stitch the heading tape just under the top edge of the valance. Turn under the ends of the tape and machine, making sure not to catch the cords. Pull up the cords to fit the board or rail and arrange the pleats.

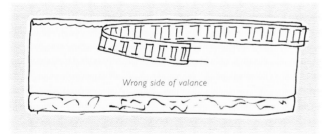

6 Simply insert hooks and hang if the valance is to be fitted to a rail. If it is to be applied to a board, you will need to stitch the soft side of the Velcro to the top of the valance. This will have to be done by hand because of the pleats. Use strong thread. Attach the other side of the Velcro to the edge of the board with tacks or staples.

IDEAS FOR VALANCES

• **Any heading used for curtains can be applied to valances. Try handmade pinch pleats or goblet headings (pages 36–7).**

• **Add a frill or fringe to the bottom of the valance.**

A pencil-pleated valance above a matching curtain.

Project 3
Swags & tails

Currently enjoying a revival; swags and tails were used a lot in the past but in the last century they went out of fashion for a while. Particularly suitable for large formal windows, they can also be adapted for use on a smaller scale.

Swags act as a pelmet (valance). They are draped across the top of the window and the tails hang down the sides or at intervals in between swags. The completed effect should be of a continuous piece of fabric draped over the top of the window, but in reality the swags and tails are made up separately. Both swags and tails are fitted to a pelmet shelf above a window.

Materials & equipment

- top fabric (see suitable fabrics and measuring up)
- curtain lining (page 27)
- old sheeting
- interlining, if used
- strip of fabric that is 7.5cm (3in) wide and the width of the swag (for binding the edge)

Suitable fabrics

Avoid fabrics which are too stiff. Soft fabrics drape much better, while plainer ones are more economical and show off the drapes of the swags well. Be careful with striped and regular up and down patterns: swags hang much better when cut on the cross (bias) and this will, of course, mean that the stripes will be on the diagonal. If you really want to use striped fabric and prefer the stripes to remain vertical, the swag could, in some cases, be cut on the straight grain, but it will not hang so well.

Swags and tails need to be lined and if they are to be hung above interlined curtains, they will need to be interlined, too. Although swags can be lined with ordinary curtain lining, tails often display their lining so it's best to use a contrasting fabric, such as plain chintz, for these.

Hanging arrangements

Making a board

1 The best way to put up swags and tails is on a wooden board, about 1.9cm (¾in) thick and 15cm (6in) wide,

above the curtains. Fix it to the wall with angle brackets. For extra stability it is advisable to have two short supporting pieces at each end.

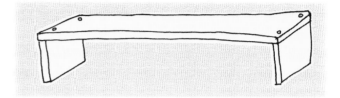

2 Staple or tack Velcro along the top of the shelf (two strips will be needed for swags and tails). The other side of the Velcro is sewn to the swags and tails and then they can be fixed simply and easily taken down for cleaning.

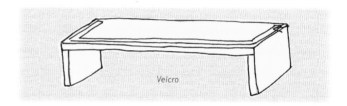

Velcro

Measuring up

The most difficult part of making swags and tails is the measuring up. It is necessary to make a template for this but there are no hard and fast rules about it. Only experience will tell you how deep you need to cut the pattern as fabrics vary so much in thickness and drapability. Here is a guide to get you started.

1 Measure the length of the board. Decide how much of this you want to be flat (unpleated) in the middle of the swag. Now drape a length of chain from one end of the board to the other allowing it to drop into a curve. Decide how deep you want this curve to be. When satisfied, measure the length of the chain.

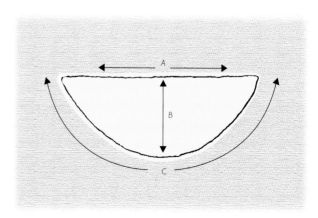

Swags need to be bound with a strip of fabric along their top edge.

2 Now make a template on strong paper. Measurement A is the amount of unpleated fabric in the middle of the swag. B is the desired depth of the swag plus the pleats (two or two and a half times the drop is usually allowed for the pleats). C is the outer edge of the curve (the measurement of the chain).

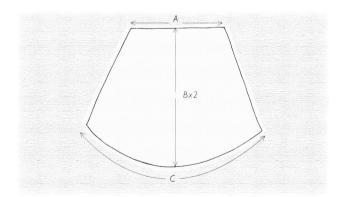

3 At this stage it is a good idea to try the shape using a piece of old sheeting or spare fabric (remember to cut the shape on the cross). Try pleating it up to see the

effect. It is useful to pin the board onto a covered board (about 10–15cm/4–6in x 1.5m/5ft long and about 1.9cm/¾in deep; covered with soft padding) so you can 'play' with the pleats. Alternatively, use the edge of an ironing board.

4 Pleat up the sides and pin in position. This is not always as easy as it sounds. Sometimes the pleats fall into position easily and other times they need to be redone several times. When satisfied, mark the position of the pleats.

Making up

1 Lay the template on the fabric and cut out the shape. Add 2.5cm (1in) for the hem at the bottom curved edge and add 3.8cm (1½in) at the top and 1.3cm (½in) at the sides. Remember the swag should be cut on the cross grain. Repeat with the lining. If interlining, see below. Lay the swag on the table, wrong side up. Turn a single hem, 2.5cm (1in), on the lower curved edge of the swag. Serge stitch in place.

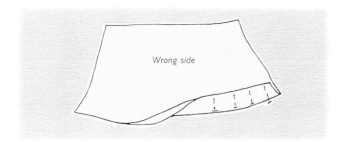

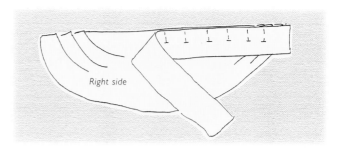

2 Lay the lining on top of the fabric, wrong sides together, with the raw edges matching up. Peel the lining back to halfway and lock stitch it to the main fabric.

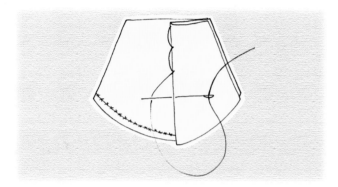

3 Turn under the lower edge of the lining and pin in place just above the edge of the top fabric. Slip stitch the lining to the hem.

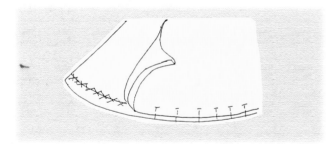

4 Tack (baste) around the other sides of the swag, then pleat the sides. You will need to repeat the process of pinning it to the board to arrange the pleats (see above) as no two fabrics behave the same. When satisfied; tack the pleats to hold in place.

5 Take a strip of fabric 7.5cm (3in) wide and the length of the pleated swag plus 2.5cm (1in). With right sides together, pin, tack and machine this band across the top of the swag using a 1.3cm (½in) seam allowance. Trim off any excess fabric.

6 Turn the band to the wrong side, then turn under 1.3cm (½in) and slip stitch the band down onto the machining by hand. Turn under the raw ends and oversew.

7 If adding braid or fringe, stitch on by hand. Stitch the soft side of the Velcro onto the band by machine. The swag is now ready for hanging. Stroke the pleats in place.

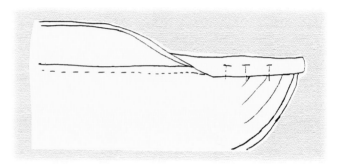

Interlining a swag

1 First, cut out the fabric and lining as above, then cut out the interlining in the same shape. All these fabrics should be cut on the cross.

2 Place the top fabric on the table wrong side up and fold up the hem. Press and then open the hem. Place the interlining on top, fold back the interlining halfway and lockstitch in place.

3 Fold back the bottom curve of the interlining and lock stitch into the fold of the hem. Trim back the interlining to 1.3cm (½in). Turn up the bottom hem and serge stitch to the interlining. Place the lining on top with the wrong side facing the interlining and proceed as before.

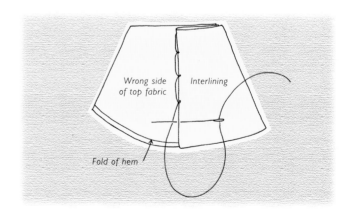

Tails

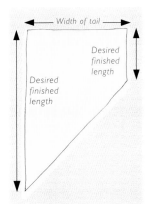

Tails are made differently from swags as the lining is an integral part of the design. The lining therefore needs to be chosen with care. A good plain chintz in a contrast colour is a safe choice. For hanging instructions, see swags, page 46.

Materials & equipment
- paper for template
- contrast fabric for lining (see Making the template)
- top fabric (see Making the template)
- Velcro

The lining of a tail is part of the design so choose with care.

Width of tail

Desired finished length

Desired finished length

Making the template
As with swags, it is a good idea to make a template for tails and also to cut out the shape in a spare piece of fabric to see the effect before cutting the real thing. Tails are easier to measure than swags. First, decide how long you want the tail to hang. This gives you the longer edge. The shorter edge is for you to decide, but it looks good if it is the same length as the swag at the point it touches. The width of the tail depends on how many pleats you want. To decide on the width of the area to be pleated, multiply by three, add any unpleated area and returns. Use the template to work out how much fabric and lining you will need. Remember, you will need a right- and left-handed one.

Method

1. Using the paper template, cut out the tails and the lining (make sure you have a right and left-handed pair!) adding 3.8cm/1½in at the top and 1.3cm/½in around three sides for turnings). Remember that unlike swags, tails need to be cut on the straight grain.

2. Place one tail on the table right side up, then place the lining on the top of the tail right side down. Pin, tack (baste) and machine around the sides and the lower edge. Take particular care across the diagonal edge, which is on the cross (bias) and will stretch and distort easily.

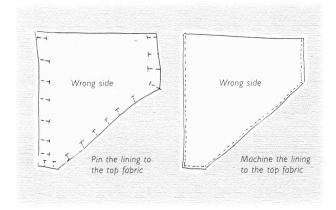

Pin the lining to the top fabric

Machine the lining to the top fabric

3. Remove the tackings and press the seam; trim the seam. Turn right sides out. Make sure the seam is on the very edge by rolling it between the finger and thumb. Press well.

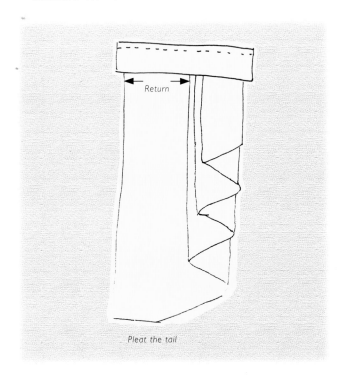

Pleat the tail

4. Pleat as required and tack in place. Take a strip of fabric 7.5cm (3in) wide and the length of the top of the pleated tail plus 2.5cm (1in). With right sides together, pin, tack and machine this band to the top of the tail.

5. Turn the band over to the wrong side, then turn under 1.3cm (½in) and slip stitch the band down onto the machining.

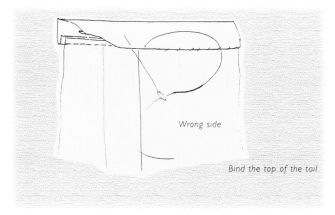

Wrong side

Bind the top of the tail

6. Turn under the raw edges of the ends and oversew. Fold the return of the tail at a right angle to the front.

7. Stitch the soft side of the Velcro to the top of the band in two pieces: one for the front and the other for the return. Tack or staple the other side of the Velcro to the top of the board. The tail is now ready for hanging.

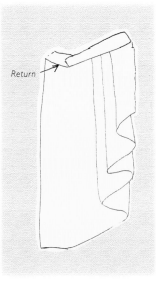

Return

> • **Swags and tails look especially good when fringing is added to the lower edge. Secure this with hand-stitching before you begin to pleat.**

Tails can be used to soften the edges of a Roman blind.

Traditional tiebacks

As their name suggests, tiebacks are used to tie curtains back! They are particularly necessary when the curtain heading is fixed and is not made to draw back on its rail. The curtains are then opened from the bottom and held back at one side, or both. Even curtains designed to draw back on their rail benefit from tiebacks as they allow the curtains to swag, giving an attractive look. They also allow more light to enter the room.

Traditional tiebacks are stiffened with pelmet buckram. They are flat and have a curved shape. They can be left plain or decorated with braid, fringe or cord. For each tieback you will need as much fabric as your paper pattern dictates (see measuring up).

Suitable fabrics
Tiebacks can be made from almost any fabric. They are often made of the same fabric as the curtain but look equally good in a contrasting material. Cord tiebacks are popular, too. With a little imagination, you can come up with lots of ideas for tying back curtains. How about rope or ribbon?

Hanging arrangements
Tiebacks usually have rings sewn onto either end and these hook over a special hook which is attached to the wall. When not in use, they remain hidden behind the curtain.

Materials & equipment
- paper for template (brown paper or pattern cutting paper)
- pelmet buckram (see Measuring up)
- lining (see Measuring up)
- interlining (see Measuring up)
- top fabric (see Measuring up)
- trimming or braid, if required
- 1.3cm (½in) brass or plastic curtain rings (two for each tieback)

Measuring up
1 To determine the required length of the tieback, hold a tape measure around one open curtain (drape) and pull the tape measure up until the desired effect is achieved.

A selection of tiebacks.

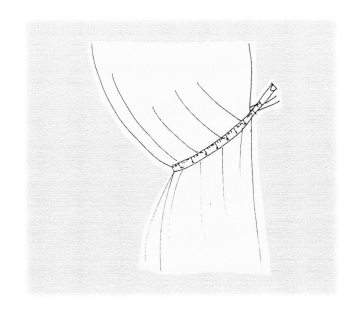

2 Take a piece of paper slightly longer than the length of the tieback and about 25cm (10in) deep. Fold in half lengthwise and draw half the tieback as shown. The tieback will sit better if it is lower in the centre than the outside edge. Round off the outer edges.

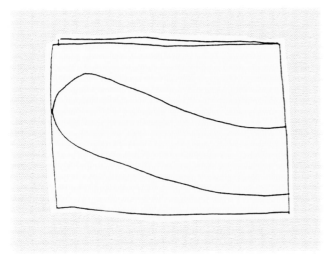

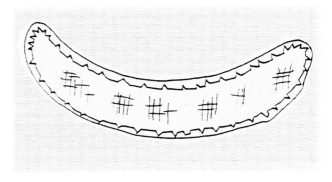

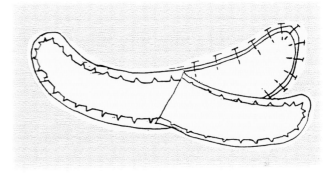

3 Cut out the complete shape in the paper and hold it round the curtain to check the effect. Adjust, if necessary. When you are satisfied with the shape, you can work out how much fabric you will need. For each tieback, you will need one piece of top fabric, plus lining, interlining and buckram. Place the template on the buckram and draw round the shape. Cut out the buckram with a pair of old scissors.

4 Using the template, cut out the lining, interlining and top fabric. The lining and interlining should be 1.3cm (½in) bigger all round than the template and the top fabric should be 1.9cm (¾in) bigger. Place the top fabric on the table wrong side up and cover with the interlining. Place the buckram on top of the interlining.

2 Take the piece of lining and place it over the exposed buckram with the wrong side of the lining touching the buckram. Turn under the raw edges and pin in place. Slip stitch the lining onto the top fabric just inside the edge.

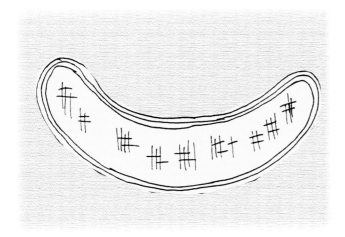

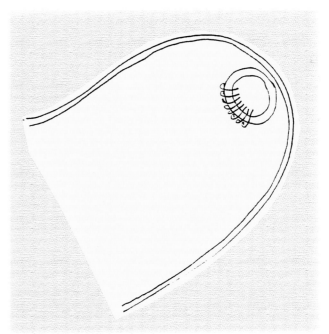

Method

1 Clip the curves of the fabric. Moisten the edges of the buckram and turn the interlining and the fabric onto it. Use an iron to press into place. Continue round until all the edges have been fixed.

3 Sew the rings onto the tiebacks using strong thread and blanket stitch. Use tiny handstitches to add braid or trimming, if liked.

PROJECT 6

Plaited tiebacks

Plaited (braided) tiebacks are fun and give an extra interest to curtains. They are also easy to make.

Suitable fabrics

Plaited tiebacks can be made of just one colour, perhaps the same fabric as the curtains, or for a livelier look, try making them in three contrasting colours. For strong contrasting colours, chintz is a very good choice, but most curtain (drape) fabrics can be used.

Materials & equipment

- fabric in three colours (see Measuring up)
- wadding or interlining (see Method)
- curtain rings (two for each tieback)

Measuring up

To determine the required length of the tieback, take a tape measure and hold it round the open curtain. Pull up until the required effect is achieved.

For a lively look, use three different colours for plaited tiebacks.

Method

1 For each tieback cut three strips of fabric one and a half times the required finished length of the tieback by 10cm (4in) wide. Press under a 1.3cm (½in) single hem, turning down one long edge of each strip.

2 Cut a piece of wadding or interlining the same width but 2.5cm (1in) shorter in length than the fabric. Place the wadding on top of the wrong side of the fabric leaving 1.3cm (½in) at either end. Roll the wadding up into a sausage shape.

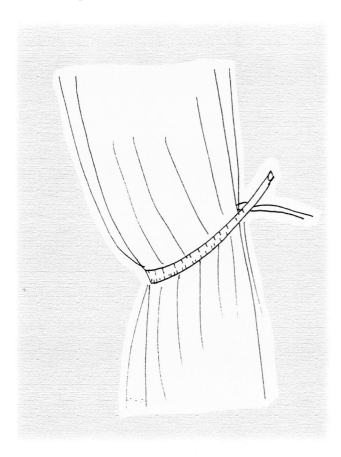

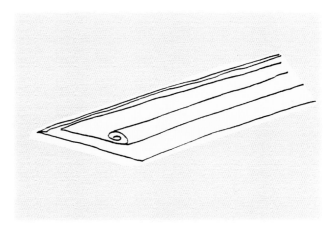

Here, the plaited tieback has been made using the same fabric as the curtain.

3 Wrap the fabric round the sausage shape, taking the turned-under edge over the raw edge. Pin and slip stitch in place. Repeat with all the strips.

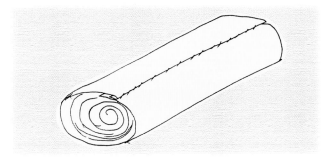

4 With the seam on the underside, pin the three 'sausages' together at one end. Stitch in place through all thicknesses.

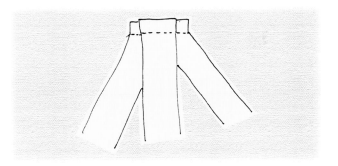

5 Now plait (braid) the three 'sausages' together. The length of the tieback can be adjusted by adjusting the tension of the plaiting. Pin the other ends together to secure. Trim away any excess and stitch across at the first end. Bind the two ends using a small piece of fabric, 10 x 5cm (4 x 2in). Place the raw edge against the raw edge of the plaited ends. Stitch across 1.3cm (½in) from the edge. Trim away any excess fabric.

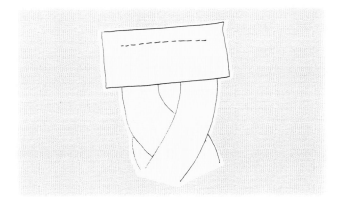

For an effective look, pick out the colours in a curtain to make plaited tiebacks.

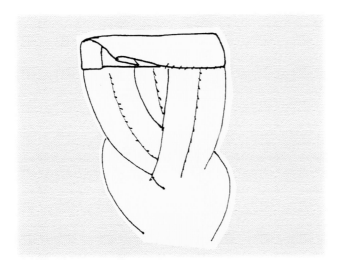

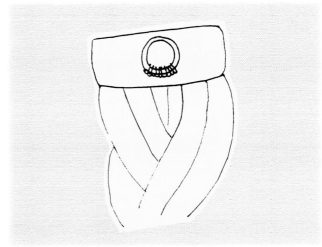

6 Pulling the seam over, turn the binding to the wrong side. Turn in the ends and the lower edge; slip stitch in place. Oversew the ends.

7 Attach a curtain ring to each end of the plaited tieback using strong thread and a buttonhole stitch.

A mix of plain and patterned fabric has been used for this tieback.

Covers

Simple throw

Throws have become very popular. This is not really surprising because they are an easy and relatively cheap way of giving a chair or sofa an instant new look. Throws can be used to hide shabby upholstery without going to the expense of a new fitted or loose cover. They can be easily washed or dry-cleaned if they become soiled. Ready-made throws are available to buy, but are sometimes quite expensive. As usual, when making your own you have a much greater choice and can also save yourself a lot of money.

Suitable fabrics

Throws can be made in almost any fabric: linen or cotton for easy washing, wool, tartan, tweed or flannel for a warmer look, or how about cashmere or mohair for the ultimate in luxury? Chenille is also a very popular choice.

Materials & equipment

2m (2.2 yards) each of 2 fabrics, each 150cm (60in) wide
7m (8 yards) of fringe or braid

Method

1 First, make sure the cut edges of the fabric are straight by laying it out on the table with the selvedges parallel to the table's edge. Allow the cut edge to hang over the edge of the table. Run a piece of tailor's chalk along the fabric hanging over the table's edge and cut the fabric along this line. Repeat at the other edge and then with the second fabric.

2 Lay one fabric on the table right side up and lay the other piece on top with the right side down. Pin and tack (baste) the two fabrics together while they are flat. Leaving a gap for turning out, machine around all four sides and then remove the tackings.

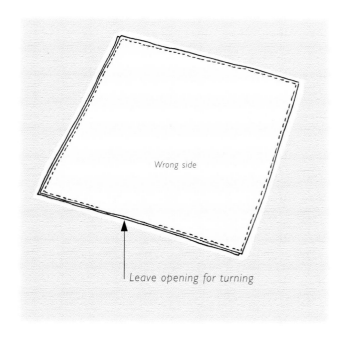

Wrong side

Leave opening for turning

3 Turn out to the right side and press. Turning the seam allowances in, oversew the gap.

4 Pin and tack the braid or fringe in position, sew either by hand or by machine, turning the cut edges of the ends of the braid under.

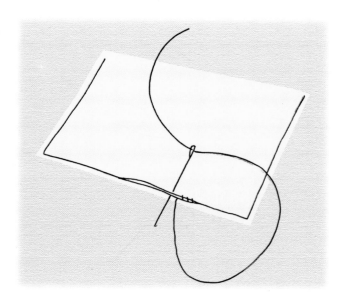

Throws can give sofas and chairs a new look.

A bobble trim added to this throw gives a stylish finish.

Round tablecloth

Tablecloths are not difficult to make. Sometimes it is hard to find them in colours to suit your taste or to match your room schemes. Making your own means you have more choice. A tablecloth can hide a multitude of sins. Who knows what is underneath? It can make a battered old table appear surprisingly smart. A cheap chipboard table, too, can be completely covered and made to look quite presentable with a floor-length cloth.

Suitable fabrics
Most curtain fabrics can be used to make a tablecloth. Brocades and silks look luxurious but, obviously, care is needed when it comes to cleaning. Cottons and linens would be more practical. Braids or fringes sewn around the edge can be added for a finishing touch.

Materials & equipment
- tailor's chalk or paper for template
- fabric (see Measuring up)
- piece of fibreboard, about 15cm (6in) square
- ball of string
- drawing pin (thumb tack)
- trimming, if used (enough to go round the circumference of the cloth)
- lining, if used (as above)

Measuring up
First, measure the diameter of the table. To make sure this is accurate, ensure the tape passes through the centre point of the table. Try several check readings!

Now measure the desired drop over the edge of the table. For a dining table this may be only a few inches – traditionally, the cloth should just reach the lap of the diner – but in the case of a chipboard table it would be better to hide the table completely by making the drop to the floor. Cloths can also look attractive if they are made longer than floor length so they are allowed to 'puddle' onto the floor.

You will need a square piece of fabric, measuring the diameter of the table plus twice the drop, plus about 5cm (2in) for turnings. This square is often wider than the available fabric width, so two lengths have to be joined

A cheap chipboard table can be completely covered with a floor-length cloth.

(top left, opposite). A middle join looks ugly so it is better to split one of the lengths and add half a width to each side of the full width. Obviously, patterns must match.

Fold the fabric in half down its length and then in half again.

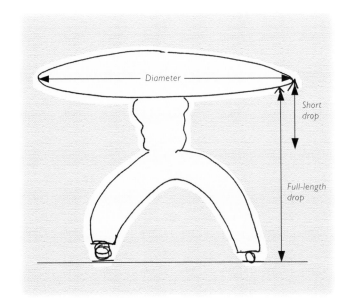

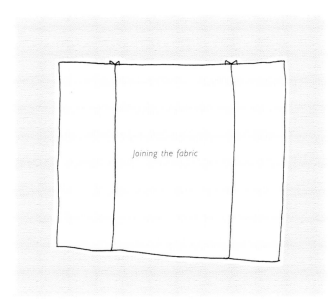

Joining the fabric

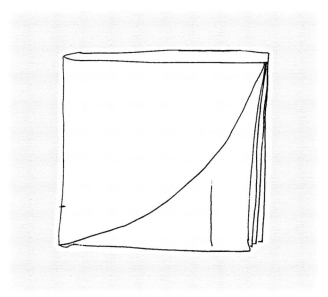

Method

1 If you are confident, draw a circle directly onto the fabric with tailor's chalk; if not, make a paper template first (Step 2). Slip a piece of fibreboard under the folded corner. Take a piece of string, slightly longer than half the planned length of the finished cloth, and attach one end to the folded corner with a drawing pin pressed into the fibreboard. Attach the other end to a pencil. Make sure the length of the string is correct for the size tablecloth proposed, i.e. half the finished length of the tablecloth plus turnings. Adjust, if necessary. Draw a quarter circle onto the fabric and then remove the string. Cut out along the pencilled line and you have your fabric circle.

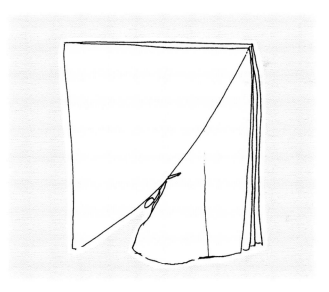

Rich red fabric complements the earthy toned ceramics.

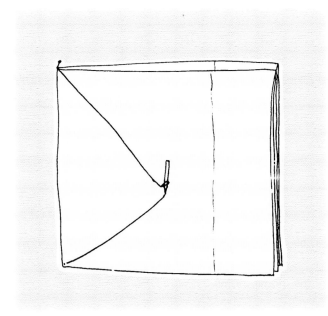

2 If you decide to make a paper template, draw a quarter circle onto a single piece of paper. Use this as a pattern on the folded fabric. Make sure that the right angle of the paper is on the folded corner of the fabric. Open out the fabric.

3 For a simple unlined cloth, turn under the hem and slip stitch around the edge. You could add a fringe or braid for extra decoration and stitch this in place by hand.

4 To make a lined tablecloth, cut out and seam as above. Cut out and seam the lining in the same manner but allow 2.5cm (1in) less all round. Turn under a single 2.5cm (1in) hem on the tablecloth. Serge stitch in place. Lay the cloth on the table, wrong side up, and lay the lining on top, wrong side down, matching up the seams. Peel back the lining to halfway and lockstitch to the cloth.

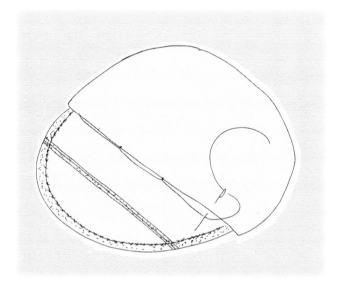

5 Repeat on the seams. Turn under 1.3cm (½in) of the lining and slip stitch the lining hem onto the hem of the tablecloth. Add trimming, if liked.

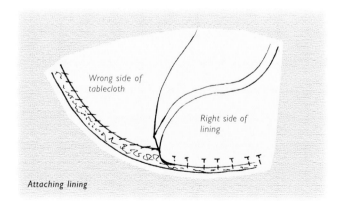

Wrong side of tablecloth

Right side of lining

Attaching lining

Dine in style with this elegant tablecloth and setting.

Detail of a corner showing the pleats.

Stools

Stools are useful pieces of furniture. They take up less space than chairs and can often be stored under tables or desks. They can also be brought out to provide extra seating when needed. Footstools are ideal for putting your feet up after a hard day's work.

Legs

These can be found at most DIY (home improvement) stores. Legs are available in a variety of styles, sizes and types of wood. They can be painted, varnished or stained to suit your own style and colour scheme.

Wood

Plywood or wood of about 1.5–2cm (⅝–⅞in) thick is suitable for the base of the stool. Obviously, a more substantial stool needs a stronger base. Most timber (lumber) merchants will be happy to give you advice and cut the wood to size.

Foam

This is available in a variety of thicknesses and densities. The vendor will be able to advise you on the best choice for your needs. It should be fire retardant.

Top fabric

You will need a good strong fabric. It could be upholstery fabric or a strong linen or cotton. The fabric must have a close weave to avoid it pulling out of shape when being made up. If you choose a patterned fabric, make sure the pattern is centralized on the stool.

Stool

Stools are quite easy to make and the end result is very satisfying. By varying the size of the top, the length of the legs and the type of fabric, very different pieces of furniture can be achieved, ranging from tiny footstools to more substantial piano stools.

Materials & equipment

- 4 legs
- piece of wood, cut to desired shape and size
- piece of foam (the same size as the wood), 7.5–10cm (3–4in) thick, cut to shape
- calico (the size of the top of the stool and 15cm/6in on all sides) plus a 15cm (6in) strip of calico, the length of the stool perimeter
- strong fabric glue
- upholstery tacks (brads) and hammer
- top fabric (the size of the top of the stool plus 15cm (6in) on all sides
- enough braid to go round the stool

Note: It is best to have the foam cut to shape professionally but if this is not possible, it is not too difficult to do it yourself. Cut a paper template, mark the pattern shape onto the foam and cut out using a sharp carving knife.

Method

1 First, make up the stool by screwing the legs to the top.

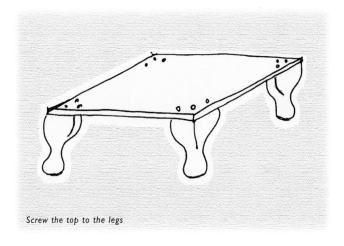

Screw the top to the legs

Stools can be made up in a variety of shapes and sizes to add an inviting look to a room.

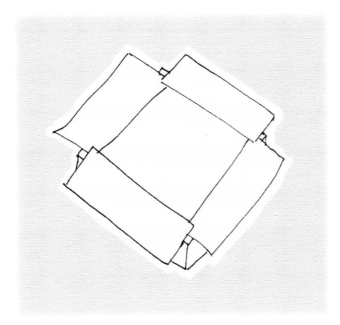

2 Place the foam in position on top of the stool. Cut four strips of calico 15cm (6in) wide and the same length as the sides of the stool. Glue one piece of calico to each side of the foam and leave to dry, as shown.

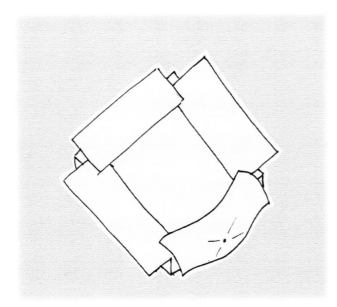

3 Starting in the centre of each side, pull the calico strips down. Hammer a tack just halfway in to hold in place at the edge of the board. Working out from the centre, hammer in a few more tacks as you pull the calico down. (Only hammer the tacks halfway in at this stage: they can then easily be removed if any adjustments are necessary.) When you are satisfied with the result and the sides are nicely rounded and smooth, hammer the tacks home and trim off the excess calico.

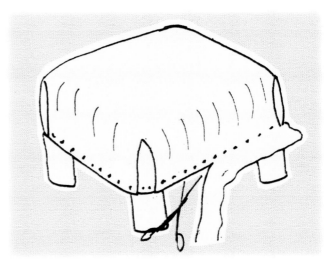

4 Place the top fabric over the foam and centralize any pattern. Starting at the centre of one side, hammer in a tack. At this stage, only hammer in the tacks halfway. Now, on the opposite side, pull the fabric down tightly and put in another tack. Repeat on the other two sides. As you do this, remove the first tacks and tighten up the fabric: it should be very tight. When you are satisfied, arrange the excess fabric at the corners into neat pleats and tack in position. Now hammer all the tacks home. Trim off any excess fabric.

5 Place braid over the tacks to disguise them. Turn in one end of the braid and tack in position. Use glue to secure the braid all round the stool. Finish by turning the raw edge under itself and putting in another tack or preferably a matching coloured gimp pin.

Use braid to cover the tack heads.

Loose covers

These can be made to cover chairs, sofas, stools and ottomans. Loose covers can be used to protect furniture from dirt and wear. Alternatively, they can give a new lease of life to an old piece of furniture by hiding shabby upholstery. New covers can be made to match a change of colour scheme in a room – a cheaper option than replacing the furniture.

As its name suggests, a loose cover is not a very tight fit and sometimes the finer details of the piece of furniture are lost under the cover. The result is a more relaxed, less formal look than a tightly upholstered piece. If you are new to making loose covers it is advisable to select something simple for your first project so you become familiar with the techniques. All chairs and sofas are different, so loose covers need to be made specifically. Each piece needs to be measured and fitted individually.

Fabrics

Strong, hardwearing fabrics which are washable are the most suitable for loose covers. Linen or linen and cotton mixes are traditionally used, but strong cotton works, too. The fabric should be smooth and tightly woven: loose weaves will pull out of shape. Plain fabrics are the most economical and are easier to make up as they have no patterns to match.

Before you start you need to make some decisions such as where to position the seams, whether or not to have a border and whether or not to have a frill.

Seams

The seams are usually placed along the outline of the chair and visible seams are often piped to add strength and give a more tailored finish.

Frills

These are often added to the base of the chair. They have the advantage of hiding unsightly legs. The alternative is to end the cover at the base of the upholstery and tie it underneath the chair, leaving the legs exposed. Sometimes the base of the chair slopes towards the back so that the back legs are shorter. Even if this is the case, the frill should still be the same height all the way round.

Types of frill

Choose from the following:
- **Gathered:** This is a pretty finish for a small chair.

The fabric must be fine enough to gather easily and hang well.
- **Box Pleats:** A more tailored frill that looks good on most pieces of furniture. It does use a lot of material, however.
- **Plain:** The simplest of all the frills, it is the easiest to measure and to make, and it looks very neat. Usually with this type of frill there is an inverted, or mock, pleat at each leg (and sometimes in the centre of a long sofa).

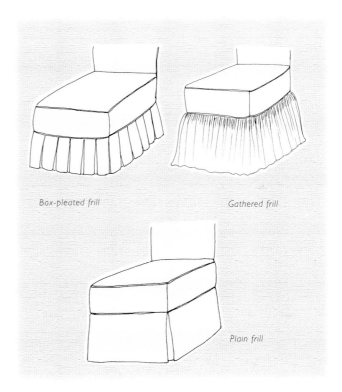

Box-pleated frill   *Gathered frill*

Plain frill

Openings

Most covers for chairs and sofas will need an opening with fasteners to allow the cover to be removed easily for washing. This can be in the form a of a placket with hooks and eyes, or Velcro or a strong zip (zipper).

Cutting out a loose cover

It is not good practice to use a paper pattern to cut a loose cover. All chairs are different and they need to be treated individually. Fabric is fitted directly onto the chair then cut out. Measure the chair parts, cut out rectangles to cover the maximum dimensions plus seam allowances and fit these onto the chair right sides out (chairs are often not totally symmetrical). The pieces then need to be pinned together following the line of the chair. Excess fabric is trimmed away, leaving only the seam allowances.

Loose cover for a chair without arms

If you have never made a loose cover before, this is a very good one to start with. You can learn all the basic techniques without things getting too clumsy or complicated. This cover has a basic flat frill with flaps at the corners designed as imitation inverted pleats.

Suitable fabrics

Fabrics for loose covers need to be very hardwearing and easy to clean, preferably washable. They are better made of closely woven fabrics which will keep their shape. Strong cottons and linens, or a blend of the two, known as linen union, are traditionally used. Plain fabric will not need to be matched or centralized, and will therefore be easier and cheaper to make up.

Materials & equipment

- fabric for the chair (see Measuring up)
- piping cord

Measuring Up

When cutting loose covers, first measure the different parts of the chair and then cut out rectangles of fabric, which are then cut to shape on the actual chair. The different parts of the chair have their own names (see below).

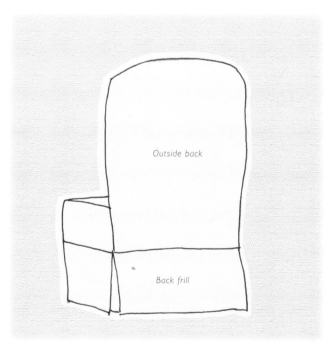

A mock inverted pleat looks smart at the corner of the frill.

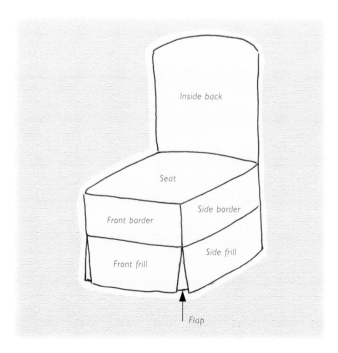

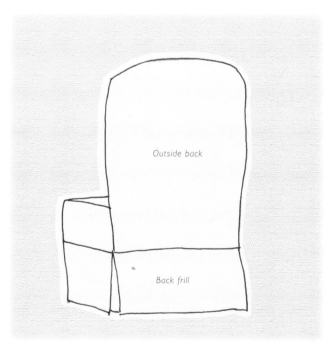

First, determine the length and position of the frill. Using a wooden or metal ruler, measure up from the floor and mark where you want the frill to start. With pins, mark this height all the way round the base of the chair even if the chair slopes down towards the back.

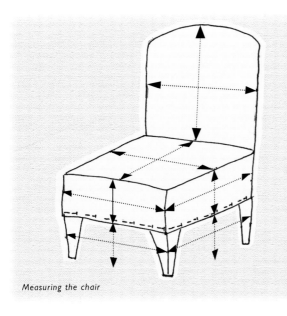

Pinning the frill height

Now measure the chair as shown in the diagrams, noting the following four points:

(i)   The inside back measurement should allow for any thickness in the chair so that the outside back is flat.

(ii) If there is a tuck-in at the back of the chair (you can feel this by pushing your hand down the back of the seat), you will need to add extra to the back of the seat and the bottom of the inside back measurements.

(iii) The length of the frill and the flaps need to be double to avoid unsightly hems. Allow 20cm (8in) for the flap width.

(iv) You need to add 2.5cm (1in) to all these measurements for the seams.

Measuring the chair

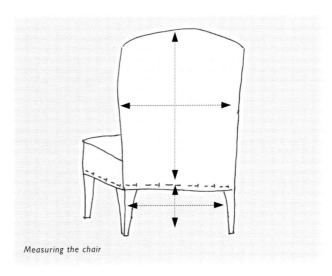

Measuring the chair

Make a plan

To work out the most economical cutting layout, you need to make a plan. Remember the grain of the fabric must always run up and down the chair and that if there is a definite pattern, it must be centralized.

Cutting out

Cut out the rectangles according to your plan. Mark each piece with tailor's chalk or a label to identify it. You might also need to mark the right and wrong side of the fabric if it is plain and not very obvious.

Making up

First, join the piping (page 85) and put in the cord ready for use later on (page 86). Measure across the inside back of the chair to find the centre line. Do this at several points and put a row of pins in to mark the centre line. Repeat on the seat and on the outside back.

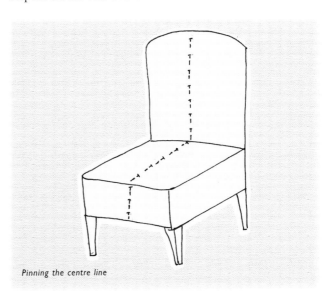

Pinning the centre line

As chairs are not always totally symmetrical, it is better to place the fabric right sides out on the chair for cutting. Take the inside back piece and fold in half along the grain, wrong sides inside. Offer it up to the back, placing the folded edge along the line of the pins.

Remove the pins on the chair and open the fabric out across the back. Pin to hold in position. (Experienced cutters will use the fabric doubled and pin only half a chair, but it is easier for beginners to cut singly.) Follow the same procedure with the seat.

Pin the outside back into position in the same way as the inside back. Now pin the outside back to the inside back following the line of the chair. You may need to make a pleat or tuck at the top of the inside back at the corners to accommodate the thickness of the chair.

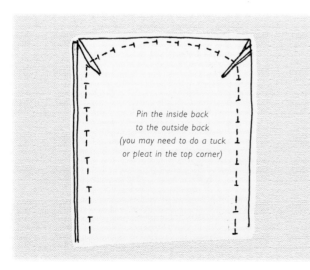

Pin the inside back to the outside back (you may need to do a tuck or pleat in the top corner)

To allow for the thickness at the bottom of the inside back, you will need to snip the fabric to turn the corner. Be careful! Almost any wrong stitching can be undone, but cutting cannot. Join the seat to the inside back.

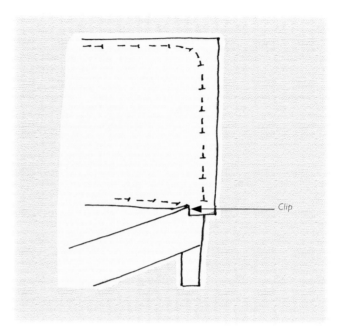

Clip

Tuck-in

Sometimes the tuck-in does not go the full width of the chair and is interrupted by the legs. In this case it is necessary to do a little cut-out as shown in the diagram.

Tuck-in

An old chair can be given a fresh lease of life with a new cover.

Border

Join the three pieces of the border together using 2.5cm (1in) seam allowances. At this stage these seams need to be machined and pressed, but do not need piping.

Starting at the centre front, pin the border onto the seat. The seams on the border should match the corners of the seat. The last few inches of the border will be pinned to the inside back. Pin the outer ends of the border to the outside back.

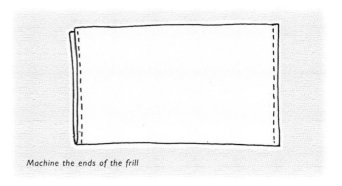

Machine the ends of the frill

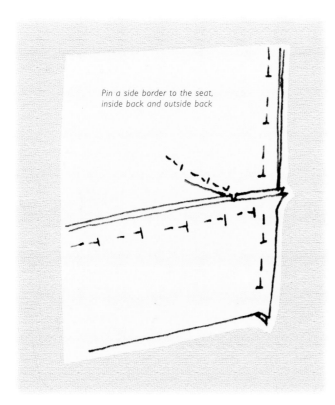

Pin a side border to the seat, inside back and outside back

Turn the cover to the right side and fit onto the chair. Press, then turn to the right side and press again. Tack (baste) the open edges of the pieces together.

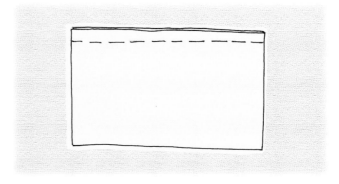

Stitch the side and front frills to the border and the back frill to the outside back, making sure that they butt together neatly at the corners. Find and mark the centre of the flaps along the raw edges and match these to the corners on top of the frill. Pin and tack in position.

Once all the pieces (excluding the frill and flaps) are pinned onto the chair, carefully cut around the shape of the chair leaving 2.5cm (1in) seam allowances. Then clip notches at regular intervals in the seams so that when taken apart the pieces can be matched again. Clip any curves and corners.

Now carefully remove the cover from the chair and unpin the pieces. Sew the piping to the relevant seams, i.e. outside back, top and bottom of the border. Now pin the pieces back together matching the notches and using a 2.5cm (1in) seam allowance. Machine in place.

Frill

Fold the pieces of frill and the flaps in half, right sides together. Stitch a 2.5cm (1in) seam down the ends of each piece.

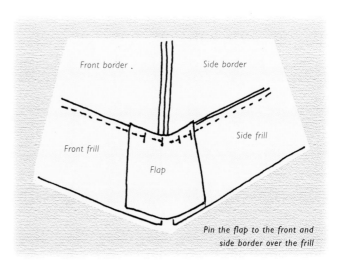

Front border *Side border*

Front frill *Side frill*

Flap

Pin the flap to the front and side border over the frill

Machine in place through all thicknesses, then neaten all seams by oversewing by hand or machine.

Loose cover for an armchair

As its name suggests, a loose cover is not a tight fit over a chair or sofa and some of the finer details of the chair are lost under the cover. However, they are extremely practical as they can be removed and washed, and can give a new lease of life to a worn chair or sofa.

Suitable fabrics

Strong, hardwearing fabrics which are washable are the most suitable for loose covers. Linen or linen and cotton mixes are traditionally used. Plain fabrics are the most economical as they do not need to be matched. This also means they are easier to make.

Materials & equipment

- fabric (see Measuring up)
- approximately 1–1.5m (1–1½ yards) of fabric for piping a chair

Measuring up

First of all you must decide:

- whether or not to have a frill
- how deep to make the frill
- to pleat or gather the frill
- whether or not to have a front panel
- the depth of the tuck-in

The tuck-in allowance is added around the seat of the chair and also between the inside back and the arms. It helps to hold the cover in place and allows the seat to give whenever anyone sits in it without putting strain on the seams. On this particular chair the inside arm goes to the top of the inside back so the tuck-in needs to be tapered at the top.

Usually a tuck-in is about 15cm (6in), but on a very deeply sprung chair it might be 23cm (9in) and on a firmer chair, less might be enough. To measure how much is needed, push your hand and tape measure down the sides of the chair.

An elderly, rather shabby chair in need of a revamp.

Method

1 First, determine the length and position of the frill. Using a metal or wooden ruler, measure up from the floor to the desired height of the frill. Mark with a pin and mark this same height all the way round the chair. Even if the chair itself slopes towards the back, the frill length should be the same all round.

Measuring the height of the frill

2 This chair has a plain frill with flaps under the corners as imitation pleats. Follow the instructions below.

Outside back　*Length*: Measure from the top of the back to the top of the frill.
Width: Measure the width at the widest part of the back.

Inside back　*Length*: Measure from the top of the back, taking in the thickness of the chair, i.e. where the outside back started, to the top of the seat. Add a tuck-in allowance to the bottom.
Width: Measure the width at the widest part. Add tuck-in allowance.

Outside arm　*Length*: Measure from the top of the arm to the top of the frill.
Width: Measure the width at the widest part.

Inside arm　*Length*: Measure from the top of the arm, taking in the thickness of the arm, i.e. where the outside arm was measured from, to the seat. Add tuck-in allowance.
Width: Measure the width at the widest point. Add tuck-in allowance.

Seat　*Length*: Measure from the back of the seat to the front edge. Add tuck-in allowance at the back edge.
Width: Measure the width between the arms. Add tuck-in allowance on both sides.

Front border　*Length*: Measure the depth from where the seat ends to where the frill begins.
Width: Measure the widest point across.

Front frill　*Length*: Measure the depth of the frill and double this.
Width: Measure the width across the front of the chair.

Back frill　*Length*: See front frill.
Width: Measure the width across the back at the frill level.

Side frills　*Length*: The same as the front frill.
Width: Measure the width of the chair at the level of the frill.

Flaps　*Length*: The same length as the frill.
Width: 15–18cm (6–7in).

Add 2.5cm (1in) seam allowances to all the above pieces.

The same chair, this time completely transformed with a new cover.

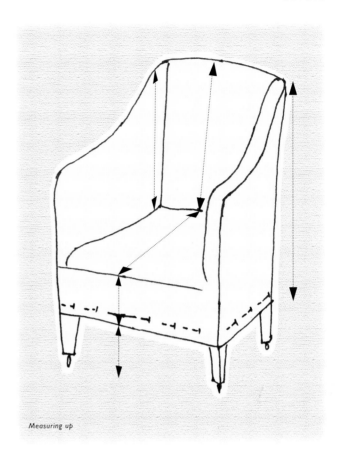

Measuring up

3 Make a layout plan of all these pieces, remembering that the grain of the fabric should go up and down on all the length measurements. You will then be able to gauge exactly how much fabric you need. Extra fabric will also be needed if designs need to be centralized.

Cutting out

Cut out the pieces as shown in the plan as simple squares and oblongs, centralizing any patterns. Do not worry about shaping at this stage: this will be done on the chair. If this is your first cover, allow a bit extra on each piece.

Cut out the piping and mark the pieces with tailor's chalk to identify them. If the fabric is plain and it is not easy to see which is the right and wrong side, mark the sides as well.

Making up

1 Now make up the piping (page 85). Measure across the inside back to find the centre. Add a pin to mark. Take several measurements and put in a line of pins down the centre line. Repeat on the seat and on the outside back. (See diagram overleaf.)

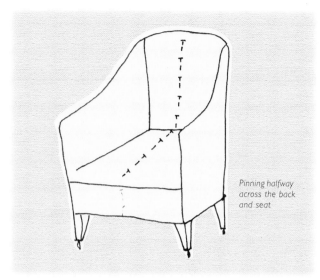

Pinning halfway across the back and seat

2 As chairs are not always truly symmetrical, it is better to place the fabric right sides out on the chair for cutting. Fold the inside back piece of fabric and then fold in half lengthwise, wrong sides together. Lay the folded edge along the line of pins.

3 Smooth out the fabric, making sure that the 2.5cm (1in) seam allowance is sticking up above the back. Pin to the chair to keep it in place. You can now remove the pins from the inside back. Open the piece out. (When you become more experienced you will be able to do the pinning with the fabric doubled and will not need to open it out.) Push the tuck-in down the seat of the chair and push any excess fabric over the arm down in between the inside back and the arm.

4 Pin the seat piece in position in the same way so that the 2.5cm (1in) seam allowance sticks out at the front

edge. Push away the tuck-ins. Now pull out the tuck-ins and pin to the inside back using a 2.5cm (1in) seam allowance.

5 Put the outside back piece in position in the same way as the inside back. Now pin the inside back to the outside back along the top, following any contours in the chair and making pleats or tucks on the inside back to accommodate shaping.

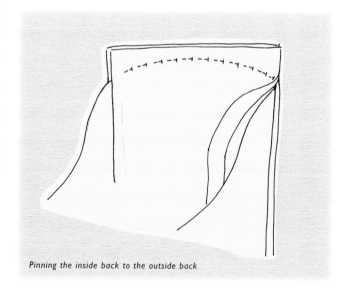

Pinning the inside back to the outside back

6 Now fit on the inside arm. Keep the grain of the fabric straight up and down. Tuck excess fabric between the inside arm and inside back down in between the two and mark the seam position with tailor's chalk. Taper the tuck-in towards the top and pin together. Cut away any excess fabric.

'Tuck-ins' around the seat and inside back allow movement without straining the seams.

7 Pin the inside arm to the seat using a 2.5cm (1in) seam allowance. Taper the tuck-in to the front edge of the chair.

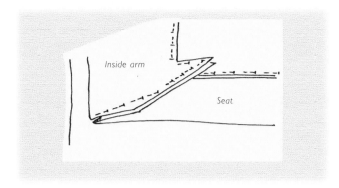

8 Pin the outside arm to the inside arm, making tucks or pleats on the inside arm to follow the shaping of the chair. Pin down the sides, joining the outside back to the outside arm.

9 Now pin the front border in position to the front edge of the seat and the outside arms. When the cover is completely pinned together (the frill is not pinned at this stage), cut all the seam allowances down to 2.5cm (1in) to follow the contours of the chair. Cut notches to show where the pieces fit together. This is very important as you need to fit the pieces together exactly as they have been pinned to get a good fit. Clip any curves.

10 Carefully remove the cover from the chair. You may need to remove some of the pins down one side of the back to allow removal of the cover. A zip (zipper) will be needed here. Take out the pins and attach the piping to the relevant seams (i.e. outside back, outside arm and front border). Machine in place. Pin the seams back together, matching notches. Tack and machine in place. Leave one side open for the zip.

11 Stitch piping to the lower edge of the cover.

12 Make up the frills and flaps by folding, right sides together, in half along the lengths. Machine the ends using a 2.5cm (1in) seam allowance.

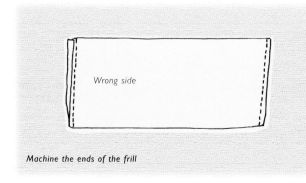

Machine the ends of the frill

13 Turn to the right sides and press. Tack (baste) together along the raw edges.

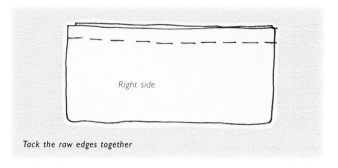

Right side

Tack the raw edges together

14 Now stitch the frills to the cover, butting the edges neatly at the corners. Fold the flaps in half to find the centre points and place them on the corners. Now sew the flaps in place behind the frill on the front corners and on the corner of the back without the zip.

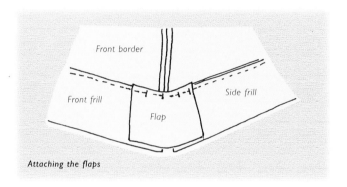

Attaching the flaps

15 Attach the flap below the zip to the side only and attach Velcro to the other side. Now sew the other side of the Velcro to the back frill.

16 Stitch the zip in place. It should start a few inches from the top of one side of the back of the chair and stop at the top of the frill.

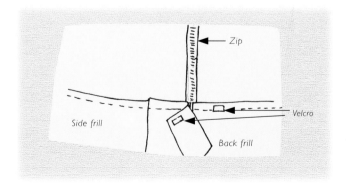

17 Neaten all the seams with overlocking, oversewing or zigzagging, then put the cover on the chair.

Cushions

Simple tassel

Tassels and cords add the finishing touches to a project. They can make a simple cushion (pillow) look quite luxurious and can be bought in many sizes and colours. Even though there is a great deal of choice, it is sometimes difficult to find just the right colour or size for your room. Making your own trimmings means you have a better chance of achieving exactly the look you want. Tassels and cords are such fun to make and the techniques are also very easy to follow – children love doing them!

Materials & equipment
- stiff card
- ball of yarn

Method

1 Cut out two rectangles of stiff card. In one dimension they should be slightly longer than the required length of the finished tassel. Wrap the yarn around the card until you have reached the required thickness. If you are making more than one tassel and they need to be the same size, be sure to count the number of 'winds' around the card so that you can repeat the thickness exactly.

A handmade tassel is easy and fun to make.

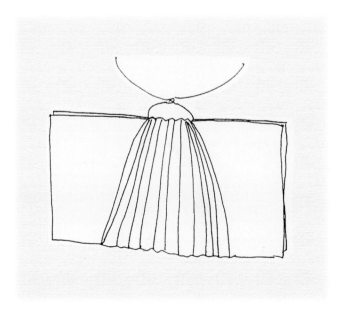

2 Take a separate piece of yarn and pass it under the wrapped thread. Pull it up to the top of the card and tie it in a reef knot to hold all the strands firmly together.

3 Pass the blade of a sharp pair of scissors between the cards and cut through the wrapped yarns along the bottom edge.

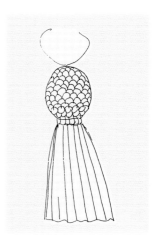

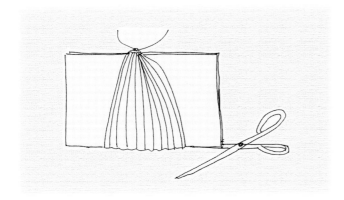

4 To form the head of the tassel, wrap another piece of yarn around the threads about one-third of the way down. Tie tightly in another reef knot.

5 To decorate the top of the tassel, thread a needle with a piece of yarn and work blanket stitch over the binding, then continue over the head of the tassel, working each row into the loops of the last. Adjust the tension to form a nice rounded head. Start decreasing as you reach the top.

Mix and match stripes and squares, but make sure the stripes line up in seams.

Piping

Piping is a folded strip of fabric which is incorporated into a seam for decoration. It can be of the same cloth or a contrasting colour. Corded piping has cord set into the fabric strip before it is stitched into the seam. It gives a professional finish to the edges of cushions (pillows) and to the seams of loose covers; it also adds strength. If piping is to go around curves or corners without wrinkling, it must be cut on the cross grain of the fabric to allow maximum stretchability. A rotary cutter and a metal ruler are very good tools for cutting bias strips accurately.

Materials & equipment
• fabric (enough to cover the piping)
• piping cord (enough to edge your chosen project)

Method
1 To cut the fabric on the cross, fold over one corner so a 90° corner is formed. Cut along the folded edge.

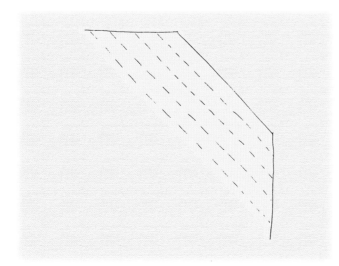

2 Cut strips parallel to the cut edge. Usually piping strips are about 3.8cm (1½in) wide but this will of course vary depending on the width of cord being used.

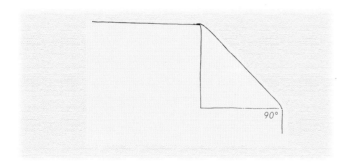

3 Now the strips need to be joined. To do this, lay two strips on the table right sides up.

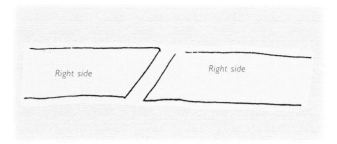

Take one of the strips and turn it over, then place it at right angles to the first strip so that the raw edges of the ends of the strips are together.

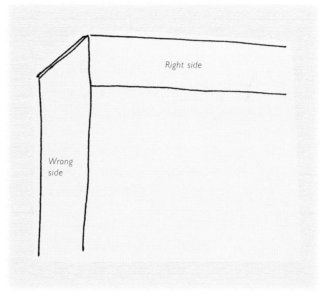

4 Now adjust the strips to resemble the diagram below. Pin, tack (baste) and machine the strips together.

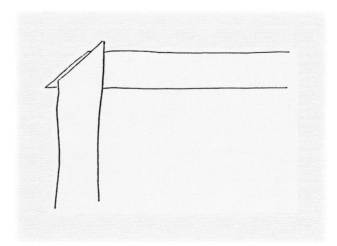

Cushions can be made up in a variety of shapes. Trimmings supply the finishing touch.

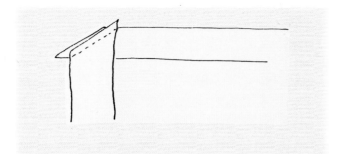

Repeat with all the strips until you have a continuous length of piping.

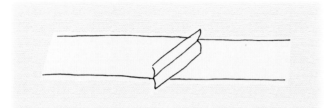

5 Now lay the piping cord on the wrong side of the strip. Fold the strip over the cord and tack, then machine in place close to the cord. A piping foot fitted on your machine is very useful for this job. It has a groove under one side of the foot that rides over the cord. Alternatively, use a zipper foot. Either foot allows you to sew closer to the cord than a normal foot. Press the seams open.

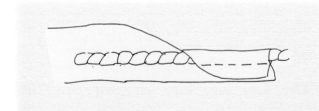

6 To sew the piping into a seam, lay the piping on the article right sides together with the machining of the piping along the stitching line of the seam. Pin, tack and machine in place close to the cord.

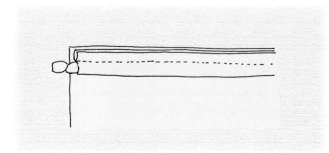

Now lay the other piece of fabric on top with the edges together to enclose the piping. Pin and tack in place.

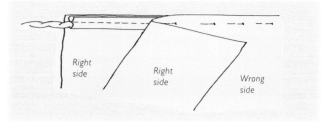

Turn the article over so that you can see the line of machining which attaches the piping. Using this line as a guide, stitch even closer to the cord to ensure a good tight fit and a professional finish.

Joining piping cord

If the corded piping is to be used around a cushion it will eventually need to be joined.

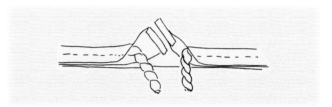

Join the piping strips as above, then join the cord. Cut the cord so it overlaps by about 2.5cm (1in). Take one end and separate the three strands making up the cord.

Cut 2.5cm (1in) away from two of the strands. Take the other end and cut 2.5cm (1in) away from another strand.

Twist the three strands back together and wind the thread around to hold them in place. (This is very fiddly.) For a shortcut, see page 99.

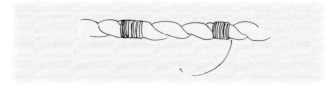

Cord

Although there are a lot of beautiful cords on the market, sometimes there is not just the right one for your needs. If you embroider your own cushion (pillow), consider using the same yarns to make a matching cord.

Materials & equipment

- ball of yarn
- 2 pencils
- a friend to help

Method

1 Cut the yarn into lengths three times as long as the required length of cord. The amount of strands depends on the required thickness of the cord and the thickness of the yarn. Knot both ends and then, with one person facing in one direction and the other facing in the opposite, each person holds one end. Stretch the yarn tightly and at each end, place a pencil between the strands, holding it close to the knot with the finger and thumb of your left hand.

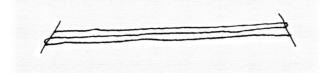

VARIATIONS

- **For a tweedy effect, try mixing different colours of cord.**

- **For a two-coloured cord, knot equal lengths of two colours together. Divide the two colours (you will need a partner for this). One person holds the centre point of one of these colours and the other person holds the centre of the other colour. Now walk away from each other until the knots are together in the middle, then continue as for the main method.**

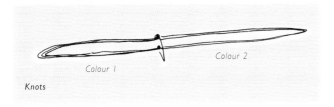

Colour 1   *Colour 2*

Knots

2 Keeping the yarn taut, each person revolves the pencils clockwise with their right hand until the threads are tightly twisted together along the whole length. Keep the twisted thread taut. One person now grips the centre of the twisted threads and walks toward the other to put the pencil ends together, then takes hold of both ends. (The threads should still be kept taut.)

3 Now, holding the two knots in one hand and the folded end in the other, let the folded edge go. The cord will form its own twist. Tie the knotted ends together firmly with an overhand knot.

Fringes, tassels and cords add a touch of luxury to cushions.

Cushion pads

Cushion (pillow) pads are available in a variety of sizes and shapes. There is usually a choice of fillings, the most popular two being curled feather or polyester. Synthetic fillings are usually better for people with allergies. For a wider choice of fillings, you can also make your own pads. These include foam chips (washable but feels a bit lumpy), kapok (soft and natural, but tends to go lumpy quite quickly), down (very light and soft, but quite expensive) and polystyrene beads (particularly good for beanbags) and finally, if you want a firm shape, foam rubber cut to size is ideal.

The fabric for the cushion pad varies depending on the filling. For foam, beans and kapok a strong cotton is satisfactory, but for feather and down it is necessary to use a down or featherproof cambric or ticking. These fabrics have been very closely woven to help prevent the feathers and down working their way through the fabric.

PROJECT 2

Make your own cushion pad

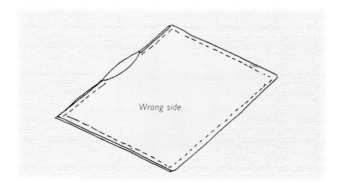

Materials & equipment

- paper for template
- 2 pieces of suitable fabric (see above), slightly bigger than the required cushion
- filling of your choice (see above)

I Make a paper template for the shape required. The cushion pad should be bigger than the finished cushion by about 2.5cm (1in) in each dimension. Use the template to cut out the shape twice in fabric. Put the two pieces of fabric right sides together. Pin, tack (baste) and machine together leaving a small opening for the filling to be added.

Wrong side

2 Remove the tackings and turn the cover right side out. Add the filling, then oversew or machine the opening. A word of warning: if you are filling the cushion with feather or down or a mixture of the two, the best place to do the filling is in the bath with the door and window firmly closed. Tack the opening of the bag which holds the feathers to the opening of the cover, making sure there are no gaps, then shake the feathers into the cushion. Remove the tackings and quickly oversew the gap with small stitches.

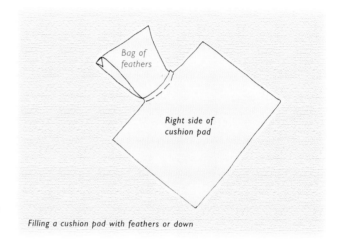

Bag of feathers

Right side of cushion pad

Filling a cushion pad with feathers or down

Cover a plain cushion pad in a warm cream fabric scattered with stars for a Gothic look.

PROJECT 3

Simple square cushion with cord & tassels

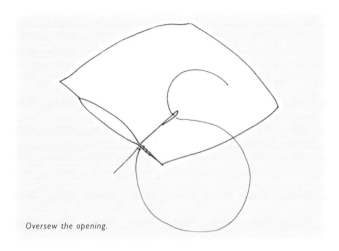

The simplest square cushion (pillow) cover has no fastening, but the opening is handstitched. When the cushion needs to be cleaned, the band stitching is simply undone. This method is unsuitable for covers which need to be washed frequently.

Materials & equipment
- square cushion pad of your choice
- paper for template
- piece of fabric (see Measuring up)

Measuring up
First, measure the pad and make a paper template exactly the same size. The cover will then be smaller than the pad, ensuring a snug fit. If you are using a fabric with a definite pattern, decide which piece of the pattern looks best when cut into a square: try to centralize any motifs.

Oversew the opening.

3 Turn the cushion cover inside out and insert the cushion pad. Turn in 1.3cm (½in) on each raw edge and oversew together. (If attaching cord, leave a small opening in the stitching of about 5cm (2in). Attach the cord by hand, slip the ends into the opening and stitch up the opening. If adding tassels (page 82), attach them securely to the corners.

A simple tassel adds interest to this plain cushion.

RIGHT: Make sure the design fits into the square.

WRONG: The design does not fit into the square.

Making up
1 Cut two pieces of fabric using the paper template.
2 Place the two pieces of the fabric right sides together. Pin, tack (baste) and machine around three cushion sides and 5cm (2in) at each end of the fourth side, using a 1.3cm (½in) seam allowance. Neaten the edges with a zigzag or overlocking stitch, or hand oversewing and fold the corners in.

PROJECT 4

Square cushion with zip

Inserting a zip (zipper) into a cushion (pillow) cover means it can easily be removed for cleaning. A zip is perhaps the most concealed fastener and the resulting cushion has very clean lines. Piping adds definition and is a smart addition.

Materials & equipment
- paper for templates
- top fabric (2 x 40cm/16in square)
- 36cm (14in) zip
- fabric or wide bias binding (for covering piping cord)
- piping cord (enough to edge the cushion)
- 40cm (16in) square cushion pad

Method

1 First make a paper template 40cm (16in) square. Place the template on the top fabric, making sure that any design on the fabric fits well into the square. This is particularly important for the cushion front, but less so for the back. Cut out two squares.

2 Make up the piping cord (pages 85–6).

3 Starting at the bottom of the front cushion piece, pin and tack (baste) the piping in position. When you reach the corner, clip the piping back to the machining. Turn the corner with the piping, clipping it open into a right angle. Continue pinning and tacking (basting), and repeat at the next corner. Complete all four corners.

Joining piping – the easy way.

4 Join the piping at the base of the cushion (see Piping, page 86), or try the following method which is easier. Straighten off the ends of the piping strip. Fold under 6mm (¼in) of one of the strips and lay it against the cushion front. Lay the other piece of piping on top. Cut the cord so that it butts up together and place on top. Now fold over the piping and tack (baste) across. Machine around the piping using a zipper or piping foot.

5 Lay the back of the cushion on top of the front, right sides together. Pin and tack the back and front together, leaving an opening at the base big enough for the zip. Machine together from the front of the cushion so that you can see the other row of machining. Machine on top or slightly inside this row.

6 Remove the tackings and neaten the raw edges by overlocking, zigzagging or by hand. Fold in the corners and turn the cover inside out. Now fold in 1.3cm (½in) of the non-piped edge of the opening. Place the zip in position under the piped edge. Pin, tack and machine along the gulley formed by the piping using a zipper foot. Place the folded edge on top of the other side of the zip and pin, tack and machine in place using a zipper foot.

7 Turn the cover inside out, neaten the raw edges by hand or machine and turn to the right side. Insert the pad and zip up.

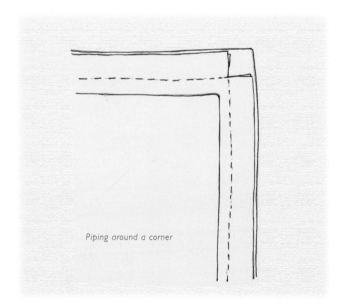

Piping around a corner

The completed square cushion in fresh checks.

PROJECT 5

Square cushion with buttons

By using buttons on this cushion the fastening becomes a feature. There are so many attractive buttons on the market now that it is difficult to choose. Try covering your own for a different effect.

Suitable fabrics

Almost any curtain fabric will be suitable for these cushions.

Materials & equipment

- paper for templates
- top fabric (see Measuring up)
- buttons
- 40cm (16in) square cushion (pillow) pad

Measuring up

1 First, make paper patterns for the back and front. The front measures 40cm (16in) square. For the back, make two paper patterns, one measuring 40 x 21.5cm (16 x 8½in) and the other measuring 40 x 33cm (16 x 13in).

2 Place the pattern on the fabric, making sure that the

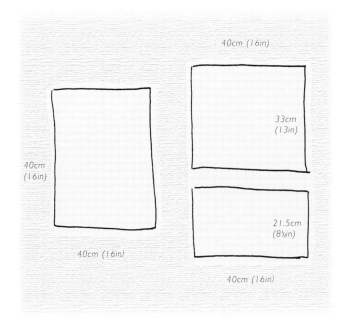

fabric fits well into the square. Press under 1.3cm (½in) on one long side of each of the back pieces of fabric, then turn under another 3.8cm (1½in).

The fastening becomes a feature when wooden toggles are applied to this cushion.

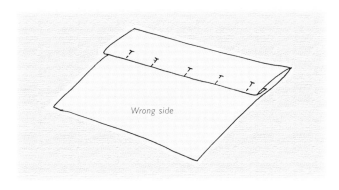

Wrong side

Method

1 Pin, tack (baste) and machine in position. Make three buttonholes by hand or machine on the smaller back piece. Sew corresponding buttons on the other back piece. Fasten the buttons to make one cushion back. The resulting square should be 40cm (16in).

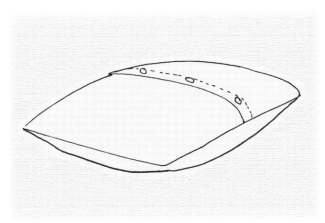

Right side   40cm (16in)

40cm (16in)

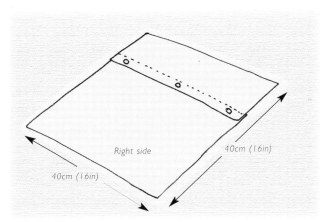

2 Place the front piece over the back, right sides together, with the raw edges matching and pin, tack and machine together. Neaten the raw edges with zigzag hand oversewing or overlocking and fold in the corners. Remove the tacking and turn to the right side. Insert the pad and button up the cushion.

Tie cushion

Instead of using the conventional zip (zipper), try fastening your cushions with ties. If you are inexperienced in putting in zips or making buttonholes, this is a good alternative method.

Suitable fabrics
Almost all curtain fabrics could be used to make these cushions but their contemporary look lends them to fairly strong cotton.

Materials & equipment
- paper for templates
- fabric (see Measuring up)
- 46cm (18in) cushion pad

Measuring up
Make paper patterns as follows:
46cm (18in) square for the front and back
46 x 18cm (18 x 7in) for the flap
5 x 30cm (2 x 12in) for the ties (cut 4 ties)
46 x 5cm (18 x 2in) for the facing

Making up
1 Place the paper patterns on the fabric (be sure to centralize any design especially for the cushion front). If using stripes, notice which way they will fall. Now cut out each of the pieces: one back, one front, one flap and four ties.
2 To make the ties, fold the cutout pieces in half lengthwise and machine 6mm (¼in) from the raw edges along the long sides and across one short edge.

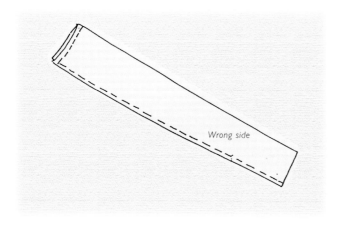
Wrong side

Ties are a good method for beginners.

3 Turn to the right side and press. Place the ties in position on the right side of the front piece 10cm (4in) in from the sides. The raw edges of the ties should line up with the edge of the front.

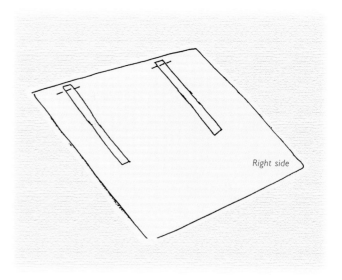
Right side

4 Take the flap piece and make a hem along one long side. Pin, tack (baste) and machine in position. Now place the flap piece on top of the front piece, right sides together, so the ties are sandwiched in between.

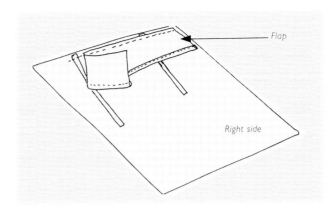

Flap

Right side

5 Pin, tack and machine the flap to the front along the long edge. Then take the back piece and place the ties in position on the right side 10cm (4in) in from the sides as for the front (see diagram, Step 3). Pin, tack and machine in place.

6 Now take the facing and place it on top of the back, right sides together, so the ties are sandwiched in between. Pin, tack and machine in place.

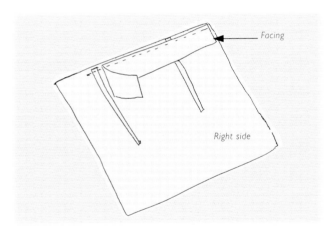

Facing

Right side

7 Turn the facing to the wrong side of the back, then turn under the long raw edge. Pin, tack and machine onto the back.

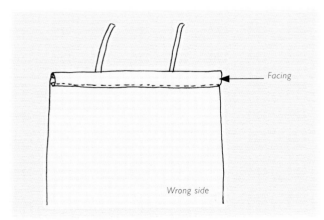

Facing

Wrong side

8 Place the front of the cushion on the table right side up (hold the flap and ties out of the way). Put the back piece on top, right sides down, with the faced edge butting up to the flap seam.

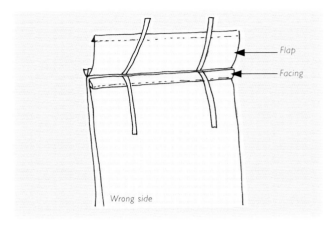

Flap

Facing

Wrong side

9 Now put the front flap over the back. Pin and tack around the two sides and the bottom of the cushion so the sides of the flap are enclosed inside the cushion sides. Machine in place.

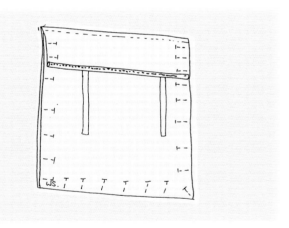

10 Neaten the seams by overlocking, oversewing or zigzagging. Remove all tacking and turn the cover to the right side; press. Place the cushion pad inside the cover and arrange the flap. Secure with the ties.

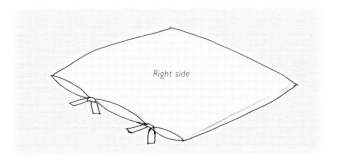

Right side

PROJECT 7

Bolster cushion

A bolster cushion (pillow) looks very smart and may seem difficult to make. Yet, really, it is very simple.

Suitable fabrics

Most curtain fabrics will be suitable for bolsters. Rich velvets and silks give an exotic eastern feel but they look equally good in fresh cottons or linens.

Materials & equipment

- bolster cushion pad of your choice
- paper for making templates
- top fabric (see Measuring up)
- zip (zipper)
- piece of foam, 1–2.5cm (½–1in) thick
- cord (optional; enough for twice the circumference of the bolster)

Measuring up

1 For the main piece, measure the length of the bolster and its circumference. Add 2.5cm (1in) seam allowance. For the ends, measure the diameter and add 2.5cm (1in) seam allowance. Make two pattern pieces in paper.

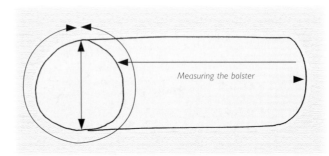

Measuring the bolster

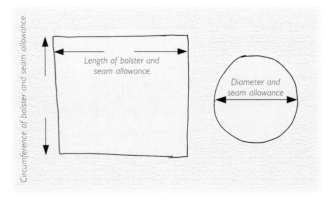

Circumference of bolster and seam allowance

Length of bolster and seam allowance

Diameter and seam allowance

2 Lay the paper patterns on the fabric, paying special attention to the position of any design in relation to the basic shape, then cut out the pieces. Cut two pieces of foam the same size as the circular ends.

Making up

1 Fold the oblong piece in half lengthwise, matching the raw edges. Pin, tack (baste) and machine 5cm (2in) in from both ends, leaving the seam open in the middle for the zip. Turn to the right side.

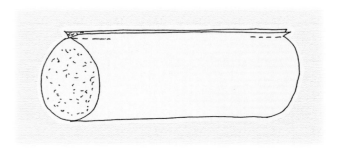

2 Pin, tack and machine the zip in place.

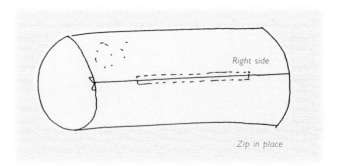

Right side

Zip in place

3 If using piping (pages 85–6), pin, tack and machine in place around the ends of the oblong piece.

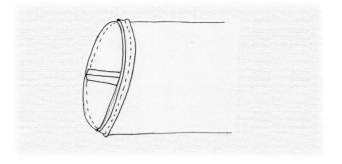

4 Divide the ends into quarters and mark these positions with pins. Now divide the circumferences of the circles into quarters. Again, pin, tack and machine the circular ends onto the main bolster piece, then clip the seams (top right, opposite).

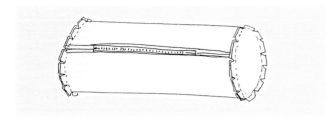

5 Neaten the seams by hand or machine. Remove all tackings and press.

6 Now turn the cushion to the right side through the zip. If using cord (page 87), stitch on by hand. Tuck the foam discs into the end of the bolster. Insert the cushion pad. Zip up.

Cord gives a tailored finish to this bolster cushion.

PROJECT 8

Box cushion

Knowing how to make box cushions (pillows) is very useful because they can be used in all kinds of situations. They are often found in armchairs and on sofas and they can also be added to window seats or garden chairs to make them more comfortable. When the chair used here was given to me, its springs had gone and the cushions were way past their best. With new springs and cushions, the chair has been given a new lease of life for very little cost.

Suitable fabrics

Fabrics need to be fairly strong and closely woven to keep their shape. Here, foam is used as a filling to give a firm tailored look. On an upholstered chair or sofa, feathers are sometimes used for a softer, more relaxed feel.

Materials & equipment
- paper for template
- fabric (see Measuring up)
- contrast fabric for piping, if required (see Measuring up)
- piping cord (pages 85–6), enough to go round the cushion twice
- zip (zipper)
- foam rubber cut to size (see Measuring up)
- Dacron wadding (optional)

Measuring up

1 Make a paper pattern the size of the cushion plus 2.5cm (1in) on the width and 2.5cm (1in) on the length for seam allowances.

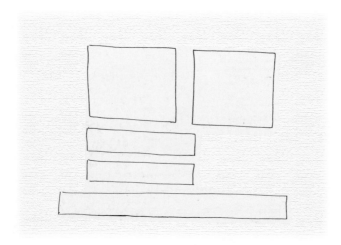

Detail of box cushion.

2 Now make another pattern for the sides of the cushion. This will be in three pieces. Each one should be the depth of the foam plus 2.5cm (1in) for seam allowances. Two of the pieces should be the length of the zip plus a 2.5cm (1in) seam allowance. The length of the third piece should be the perimeter of the cushion minus the length of the zip plus 2.5cm (1in) seam allowance. If you need to join this strip, do so at the corners of the cushion. The zip length is the length of the back of the cushion plus 20–25cm (8–10in) which makes the cushion easier to insert and remove.

Method

1 Place the pattern for the top of the cushion on the fabric making sure any design on the fabric is centralized and the sides of the pattern are parallel to the selvedges. Pin in position. Repeat with the underside pattern. Now position the pattern for the sides. These can go across or along the grain of the fabric depending on the effect required, but they must all go the same way. Then cut out all the pieces.

2 Cut out the piping. Make up the piping (pages 85–6). Starting in the middle of the back edge, pin, tack

(baste) and machine the piping in place until you reach the first corner. With a pair of sharp scissors, snip the piping up to the machining, then turn the corner with the piping. The snip in the piping should open up into a right angle. Continue tacking the piping onto the fabric, treating each corner in the same manner.

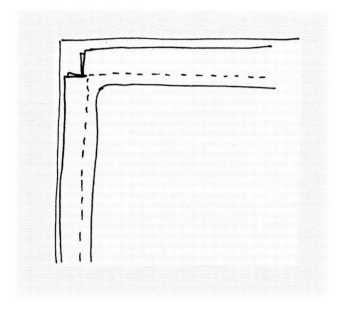

3 When you reach the beginning again, join the piping. This can be done by using the method on page 86, but an easier way is as follows: straighten off the ends of the piping strip. Fold under 6mm (¼in) of one of the strips and lay it against the cushion front. Lay the other piece of piping on top. Cut the cord so it butts together and place it on top. Now fold the piping over the cord and tack across. Machine the piping in place using a piping foot or a zipper foot.

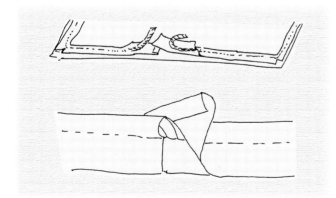

4 Take the two zip length pieces for the sides of the cushion and fold in half lengthwise with the wrong sides of the fabric together. Press.

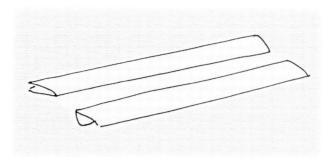

5 Open the two pieces out and place them together with the right sides of the fabric facing each other. Tack together along the centre fold.

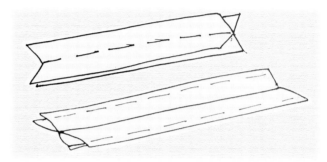

6 Refold the two pieces and tack the raw edges together. Place the zip behind the tacked seam and pin in place.

A good sand and polish, and the addition of two new cushions gave this chair a fresh look.

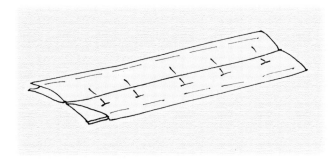

7 From the right side, tack the zip in position making sure the zip teeth are centred behind the seam.

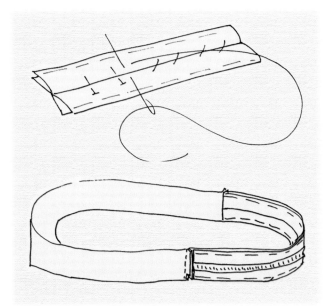

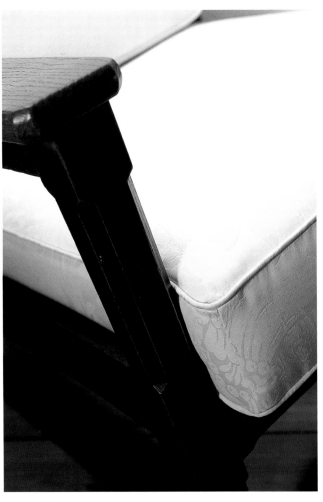

Detail of box cushion.

Machine or hand sew the zip in place then remove the tackings around it. Join the other long side piece to the zip piece along the short ends.

8 Open the zip a little way, then join the sides to the top of the cushion. Starting at the centre of the back, pin and tack the side to the top, stopping at the corner (you will need to make a little snip in the side piece to allow it to open into a right angle to go round the corner).

Treat all the corners in the same way. Repeat with the base of the cushion and machine the sides to the top.

9 Neaten the raw edges with overlocking, zigzag or hand oversewing, then remove all the tackings. Open the zip and turn the cushion the right way. (If you prefer a softer shape for your cushion, wrap the foam in Dacron wadding. Just stitch roughly to hold in place.) Slip the cushion pad inside.

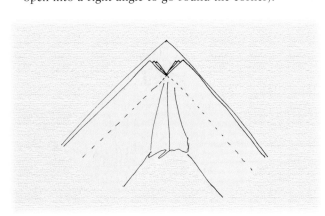

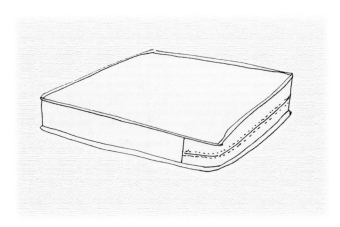

The box design works well in classic cream.

Care of soft furnishings

With a little care and attention, your soft furnishings should look good for a long time. Here are a few hints to keep them looking their best.

Curtains

Direct sunlight is probably the one thing that does the most damage to curtains (drapes) and soft furnishings so try to protect them against this, or fabric will fade and eventually rot. Lining curtains helps protect the top fabric from the sun and, even if the lining rots, the curtains can be relined for a fraction of the cost of replacing them with new ones. Consider fitting a blind (shade) at a south-facing window and keep it closed during sunny days when you are out.

Avoid touching or handling curtains, even with clean hands. Your hands are naturally oily and will soil curtains. To avoid touching curtains, fit pull cords. The added advantage of these is that curtains can be drawn by their headings, whereas pulling them from lower down can distort them. An alternative to a corded rail is a long rod which hooks into one of the gliders and can be used to draw the curtains.

Vacuum curtains regularly on minimum power. Make sure you get between the pleats and right into the folds. Curtains should not need to be cleaned too often. To prepare them for cleaning, take them down and if they have machined headings, undo the cords and release the pleats. Dry-cleaning is the safest (and most expensive) option, but if you are prepared to take a risk and you are sure the fabric is washable, gently soak the curtains in lukewarm water and mild detergent, being careful not to agitate them too much (the bath is a good place to do this). Rinse and hang out to dry. Avoid tumble-drying as it might cause shrinkage.

Loose covers

Like curtains, these, too, are susceptible to damage from direct sunlight so bear this in mind when positioning your furniture. Clean loose covers regularly with a vacuum cleaner, pulling out and shaking any tuck-ins, where crumbs and dust like to hide. The arms of chairs and sofas are the most likely parts to soil and wear out. For this reason, it is a good idea to make extra arm covers in the same fabric to protect them. These can easily be removed for washing.

When a cover needs cleaning, undo the fasteners and remove from the chair or sofa. Dry-clean or wash gently according to the fabric. Iron any frills and large areas. Refit the cover when it is slightly damp to pull it back into shape and if necessary, press in position.

Stools

Spray stools and fitted upholstery with Scotchguard to help protect them from excess dirt.

General advice on washing fabrics

To prolong the life of fabric, gentle washing is always recommended. Very hot water and rough treatment can damage articles. Many washing powders contain bleach, which is fine for white fabrics, but they may also whiten cream fabrics and lighten coloureds, so choose a detergent designed especially for coloureds. Biological powders are very good for removing food or bloodstains and there are special detergents on the market for silks and wools.

Removing stains

Stains are best dealt with immediately since the results are much more likely to be effective.

- **Blood** If just a small area has been stained, or if you prick your finger while sewing, put a little of your saliva onto a cotton bud and gently rub on the mark. For larger areas, wash with a biological detergent.
- **Candle wax** Scrape away the excess wax and sandwich the stain between blotting paper or clean white paper, then press with a warm iron. Repeat, if necessary. Finally, clean with a grease solvent.
- **Coffee & tea** Mop up immediately with a clean cloth or paper towel. Dab the area with a wet cloth soaked in dilute detergent.
- **Grease** Scrape off the excess and treat with a grease solvent.
- **Wine** Mop up the excess wine immediately and then cover it with salt to soak up the stain. Leave, preferably overnight, and if necessary, wash with a biological detergent.

Fabric directory

Brocade is a self-coloured fabric with a pattern formed in the weave on a Jacquard loom. The pattern is made using a satin weave, which appears alternately on the face and reverse of the fabric. Patterns are traditionally flowers, leaves and birds. Brocade was originally made of silk, but is now often made from synthetics.

Buckram is a stiffened fabric. Heavy pelmet buckram is made from hemp; lighter versions are made of cotton.

Bump A delightful name for this thick fleecy fabric which is used for interlining.

Calico is a cheap woven cotton originating from Calicut in India. It is usually sold unbleached and undyed, and so is a creamy colour. Calico is available in several widths and thicknesses.

Cashmere is a luxurious and expensive fabric. Made from the hair of the Cashmere goat, it is recognizable by its smooth soft finish. It is very light, but very warm.

Chenille With its soft velvety pile, chenille is made from hairy threads resembling caterpillars, hence its name, which is French for caterpillar. It is usually synthetic.

Chintz was traditionally a patterned cotton, sometimes glazed and usually made up of large designs of birds or flowers. It has now come to mean a glazed, often plain coloured, cotton.

Cotton is a natural fibre made from the cotton plant. It has been produced for thousands of years. The quality depends on the length of the fibres: the longer the fibre, the better the cotton will be. Sea Island and Egyptian cottons are considered the finest. Cotton can be woven into many different fabrics of diverse weights and thicknesses.

Domette is a thick fleecy fabric used for interlining.

Dupion is a silk fabric with a slubbed weave originally caused by two silk worms getting too close and spinning their cocoons together. It is relatively inexpensive.

Linen is a strong hardwearing fabric made from the stem of the flax plant.

Mohair, a natural fabric, is made from the hair of the Angora goat. It tends to be hairy, but is very warm.

Muslin, or butter muslin as it is often called, is a light, loosely woven cotton fabric originally used to strain milk for making butter. It is very cheap.

Sateen is a cotton fabric with a satin weave, which gives it a smooth, shiny finish.

Silk, a product of the silkworm, can be woven into a variety of beautiful fabrics.

Velvet can be made from cotton, silk or synthetics. It has a cut pile, which gives a luxurious finish.

Voile is a fine, even weave fabric traditionally made from cotton but now also from synthetics.

Wool is another natural fibre that is made from the fleece of sheep. It is a very warm fabric.

Glossary

Bolster   A cylindrical cushion.

Bump   Thick cotton fabric used for interlining curtains.

Curtain lining   Special fabric made of cotton sateen. It is available in many colours.

Cushion   A stuffed pad used on chairs or sofas for decoration and comfort.

Goblet pleats   Handmade curtain heading. The pleats are evenly spaced and resemble goblets.

Heading tape   Tape stitched to the top of the curtain to form a heading. Some of the headings are corded and the cord can be pulled up to form pleats or gathers. Some heading tapes have pockets to hold the hooks for hanging the curtains.

Interlining   An extra layer of fabric used in interlined curtains between the top fabric and the lining.

Loose cover   A shaped cover for a chair or sofa which is easily removed for cleaning.

Pattern repeat   The distance between a particular point on the pattern and the next identical point along the length of the fabric.

Pencil pleats   A type of curtain heading. The pleats lie together in parallel rows resembling a line of pencils.

Pinch pleats   Another curtain heading. This time, the pleats, each one three pleats in one, are evenly spaced at intervals.

Piping   A folded strip of fabric sewn between `seams for decoration. It is often corded, in which case it adds strength to the seam.

Piping cord   Special cord used inside piping.

Pressing   This is not the same as ironing. The iron is lifted and put down, but not moved along the fabric. Usually, a pressing cloth is used between the iron and the fabric. This can be made of muslin or a piece of fine linen.

Return	The space between the outside edge of the front of the curtain rail or pelmet board and the wall if they are not flat against the wall.
Roman blind	When down, this blind has a flat finish but it is pulled up by cords into horizontal pleats.
Selvedge	The edge of the fabric lying parallel to the warp threads. The weft threads wrap around this edge so it does not fray.
Sheers	These are made from fine fabrics which allow light to filter through them.
Straight grain	The direction of the fabric running parallel with the selvedge.
Swags	Fabric drapes which hang above curtains.
Tab tops	A simple curtain heading. Strips of fabric are made into loops which hang over the curtain rail. No hooks are needed.
Tacking	Temporary stitch used to hold fabric pieces together before the permanent stitching.
Tacks	Small metal nails with large heads.
Tailor's chalk	A special chalk used for marking fabric.
Tails	These are usually hung with swags. While swags hang across the window, the tails hang down the sides of them.
Tassels	An ornamental bunch of threads tied together in a decorative way.
Throw	Informal, two-dimensional cover used over a chair or sofa.
Tuck-in	A tuck-in on a loose cover is the extra fabric which is tucked in between a sprung chair seat and the back and arms. This allows the seat to depress without splitting the cover.
Valance	A soft frill which hangs above a curtain.

Stitch directory

Different stitches serve different purposes and it is important to use the correct stitch for the correct job.

Some stitches are stronger than others, some are almost invisible, while others are meant to be seen.

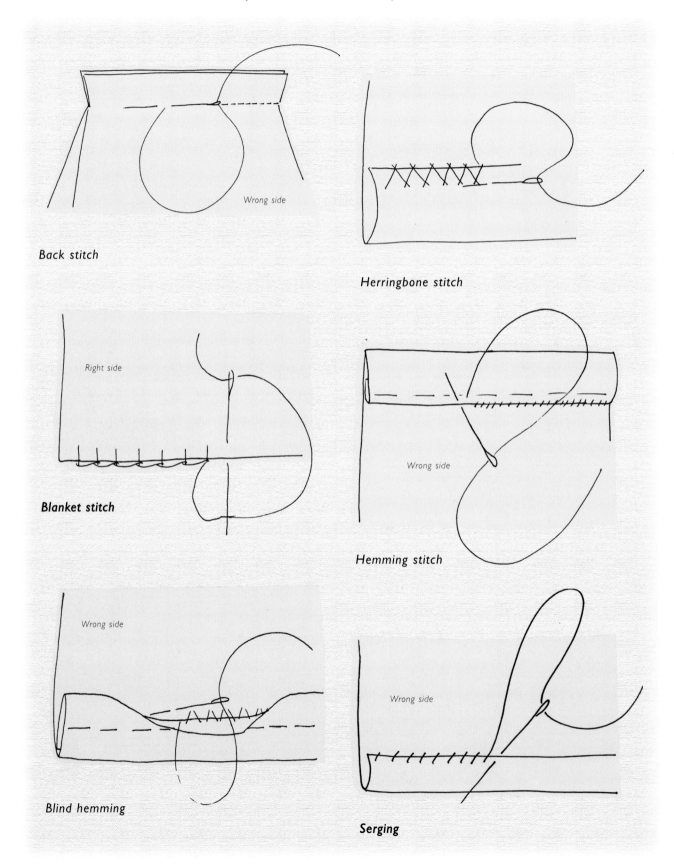

Back stitch

Wrong side

Herringbone stitch

Blanket stitch

Right side

Hemming stitch

Wrong side

Blind hemming

Wrong side

Serging

Wrong side

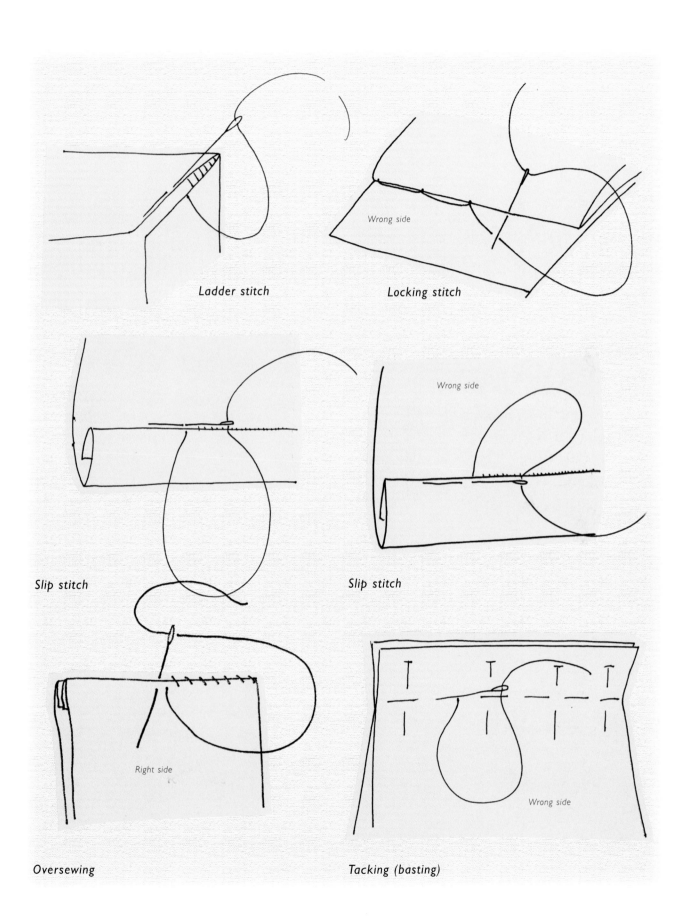

Ladder stitch

Locking stitch

Wrong side

Slip stitch

Wrong side

Slip stitch

Right side

Oversewing

Wrong side

Tacking (basting)

Stockists & suppliers

Jane Churchill
151 Sloane Street
London SW1X 9BZ
Tel: 020 8877 6400 (for stockist information)

John Lewis plc
Oxford Street
London W1A 1EX
Tel: 020 7629 7711
(branches of John Lewis throughout the UK)

KA International
42 North Street
Bishop's Stortford
Herts. CM23 2LR.
Tel: 01279 755758
www.quality-fabrics.net

Mulberry
219 King's Road
London SW3 5EY
Tel: 020 7352 1937
www.mulberry-england.co.uk

Osborne & Little
(showroom for stockists of Liberty furnishing fabrics)
304–308 King's Road
London SW3 5UH
Tel: 020 7352 1456
www.osborneandlittle.com
oandl@osborneandlittle.com

USA
Mulberry (showroom)
Long Island
201 Central Avenue South
Bethpage
NY 11714
Tel: (516) 752 7600

*Delicate beads added to sheer curtains give a
charming finish.*

Index

Acknowledgements

The author would like to thank Venetia Penfold, who first had the idea for this project; Jane Donovan, Tina Persaud, Simon Rosenheim and all the wonderful team at Batsford, who have been so kind and helpful; Michael Wicks for the use of his house and the care and patience he took with the photography; Jane Churchill and Mulberry for supplying fabrics; Elaine van Marle and Henry Collett from KA Fabrics in Bishop's Stortford, Herts., who kindly lent fabrics and samples, and lastly, her very special family.

The publishers would like to thank Michael Wicks for his beautiful photography, Brian Flynn for his inspired design and Alison Leach, editor extraordinaire.